A
BETTER
WAY *to*
THINK

Also by H. Norman Wright

Making Peace with Your Past

Finding Freedom from Your Fears

Always Daddy's Girl

The Complete Book of Christian Wedding Vows

A Dad-Shaped Hole in My Heart

Helping Those Who Hurt

The Perfect Catch

The New Guide to Crisis & Trauma Counseling

Recovering from Losses in Life

A
BETTER
WAY *to*
THINK

How Positive Thoughts Can
Change Your Life

H. Norman Wright

SPIRE

Published by Revell
a division of Baker Publishing Group
P.O. Box 6287, Grand Rapids, MI 49516-6287
www.revellbooks.com

Spire edition published 2015

ISBN 978-0-8007-2337-8

Printed in the United States of America

17 18 19 20 21 22 23   14 13 12 11 10 9 8

Contents

Introduction

I've met only a few people in my life who don't want to change. Most really do. They can envision the progress they want to make. Their intentions are good.

But there's one nagging reason that keeps many of us from moving ahead in life. It's our thoughts: those seemingly insignificant sentences that pass through the mind, greatly influencing everything we say and do. From our thoughts, we hear messages that can propel us toward great accomplishments and positive change . . . or drag us into a negative spiral.

Do you struggle with your own thoughts? Thoughts of worry, insecurity, frustration, and even anger? I do. We all do.

For many of us, the thoughts that continually run through our mind are more adversary than ally. Left unchecked, our "thought life" can become our own worst enemy, poisoning us from within. And it's our choice.

Surprisingly, many of us don't see the relationship between our thoughts, our feelings, and the words that flow from our mouth. For so many of the individuals and couples I've counseled, their difficulties can be traced back to one root problem—the ideas they repeat to themselves, their "self-talk."

Yes, it's true we all "talk" to ourselves. I do. You do too.

We all carry on conversations with ourselves. And it's really okay. It's not a sign we're going over the edge.

Sometimes, we're simply rehearsing conversations. At other times, we're letting our imagination gallop along unrestrained, building tension and anxiety by worrying about possibilities that may never occur, and might not even be reasonable to consider, but telling ourselves that danger looms. It can be a self-fulfilling prophecy. What we tell ourselves, we can make come true—even if it's something we'd desperately rather avoid.

Truth be told, most of us have a bent toward negative or toxic thinking. And for some of us, the mind is a downright dangerous place, a battlefield fraught with land mines and hidden enemies poised for ambush. Our self-talk is attacking us from within.

It doesn't have to be that way.

You can change your thoughts. I can teach you. And when you learn to control your self-talk, you'll be on your way to changing your life and improving your relationships. It's possible. Really. The practical, simple steps you'll find in this book will make a difference. What's more, you'll build a foundation for new thinking based on the Word of God. Get ready—you're on your way to the ultimate mental makeover.

As you work through this book, I pray you'll develop a new pattern of thinking, one that is balanced and realistic. My hope is that you'll discover how to make peace with your mind, allowing you to make the most of all God has for you.

—H. Norman Wright

My Mind Is Filled
with Thoughts!

No matter what the weather, Melanie radiates sunshine. At the grocery store, she makes friendly small talk with the cashier. When working in the yard, she always raises her eyes at the sound of an approaching car and waves, flashing a bright smile as neighbors drive by. Sure, she has bad days now and then. But she bounces back quickly after unpleasant events or periods of stress. Nothing seems to keep her down for long.

It's no act. Melanie really does see a blessing in almost everything. When she gets stuck in a traffic snarl that might leave others seething, she tells herself it's simply an opportunity to have some uninterrupted prayer time. If she burns dinner, she tells herself that she was due for a fun night out at a favorite eatery. Rained-out picnic plans cause her to announce that it's the perfect opportunity to gather the family around the TV for a cozy afternoon watching a movie and munching popcorn.

When a problem erupts in her life, her mind spins into solution-finding mode. She's not prone to worry. Things are probably better than they seem, she often tells herself. And usually, she's right.

Things always seem to work out for Melanie. So why can't my life go like that? Rhonda often wonders. The two have known each other since elementary school and have attended the same church ever since, serving together in countless ministries since they were teens.

She always has energy, and never even gets sick! muses Rhonda. And I'm always battling allergies, fatigue, or a cold.

The truth is, Rhonda has always found Melanie's can-do spirit a little annoying. Actually, really annoying. No one can be *that* happy, Rhonda pouts on days when the two serve coffee together at church.

Rhonda has a comfortable life—her husband makes a far bigger salary than Melanie's, and she doesn't have any real problems. Still, she feels gloomy a lot. And, she admits to her husband from time to time, she probably spends more time than she should fretting about imagined problems that never materialize.

But I can't help it, she tells herself.

She's tried the whole "don't worry until you really have something to worry about" approach. But that just seems so irresponsible.

What if we catch that really nasty flu that's going around, right before our vacation? she frets. What if the dog works his nose under the loose board on the fence, and gets out and gets hit by a car while I'm at the store? What if there's a downturn at Rob's business, and he loses his job? We could lose the house! Our savings! Everything!

What-ifs whirl through her head throughout each day. And she never really feels good anymore, though her doctor can't find anything wrong with her.

Swirling in Thoughts

Thoughts—optimistic, pessimistic, and everything in between—flit through our minds all day long. And they affect everything about us, from our emotions to our health. Melanie's cheerful, positive thoughts influence just about every part of her life, from her attitude and mood to her health—and there's science to prove it.

Rhonda's negative thoughts affect her more than she realizes—stealing her joy, damaging her relationships, even damaging her health. There's science to prove that too.

Like these two women, we're constantly processing thoughts. We couldn't possibly count the number of thoughts we have each day. There are far too many. Would you guess a thousand? Five thousand? Ten thousand? Depending on how active your mind is, you may produce more than 45,000 thoughts a day. Whew! It might be compared to a flock of birds flying in and out of your mind.

The rate at which we can express those thoughts is far slower. Some research suggests we speak at about 200 words per minute. But we can listen to and process 1,300 words per minute!

This barrage of thoughts can overwhelm us. Sometimes it seems we can't process them all fast enough. Sometimes we know what we're thinking, but can't form the words to express those ideas. Sound familiar?

So what exactly *are* thoughts? Well, they're the ways in which we're conscious of things. They're made up of our memories, our perceptions, our beliefs. They're glimpses, even snippets, of ideas. They make up one of the most basic facets of life.

> Depending on how active your mind is, you may produce more than 45,000 thoughts a day.

Sometimes they pass fleetingly, barely noticed. Sometimes they come sharply into focus. We often voice them, saying things like, "I thought of you yesterday," or "I was just thinking of our meeting tomorrow."

Our thoughts determine the orientation of everything we do. They evoke the feelings that frame our world and motivate our actions. And they have the power to change the way we feel.

Melanie's sunny thoughts shine through in her mood. She's optimistic most of the time, even when problems arise. Life just feels good to her.

But for Rhonda, even when life offers smooth sailing, she rationalizes the possibility of storm clouds forming just beyond the horizon. Worry gnaws at her as she remains on the lookout for potential problems.

Think about this: You can't evoke thoughts by *feeling* a certain way. But you *can* evoke and, to some degree, control feelings by directing your thoughts.

So having control over our own thoughts gives us power to direct our feelings. But our feelings aren't directed solely by will. We can't just choose our feelings. Still, we *can* guide them with our thoughts.

That's important because our thoughts are the origin of our behaviors. Each behavior begins this way: A thought stimulates an electrochemical response, which produces emotion; emotion results in an attitude; attitude produces behavior. This process affects the way we think and feel physically. So negative or toxic thoughts produce toxic emotions. Those produce toxic attitudes, which result in toxic behavior.

Our ability to think and represent things to ourselves also enables us to bring vast ranges of reality—and nonreality—into our lives. Basically, that means that with our thoughts, we can usher good or bad things into our lives, real or imagined, depending on the content of our thoughts.

Welcome to Thought Chemistry 101

Are your thoughts harmless or harmful? Well, it depends.

It's important to understand that our thoughts aren't isolated or disconnected. Each time you have a thought, it triggers an electrochemical reaction in your body, whether you're aware of it or not.

That's right, each thought sets off a biological process—about 400 billion at once. Because of that thought, chemicals surge through the body, producing electromagnetic waves. Those set off emotions, which affect how we behave.

We listen to our emotions and act upon them. For instance, when we're fearful or worried, we may act by withdrawing, or attacking, or blowing a situation out of proportion.[1] Whenever you have a thought, and that electrical transmission goes across your brain in a fraction of a second, you become aware of what you're thinking.

> Each time you have a thought, it triggers an electrochemical reaction in your body, whether you're aware of it or not.

Ever wonder, when you're feeling good, why you're feeling so good? Why you're feeling positive or happy? There's a simple reason for this. It's due to those chemical reactions set off in your brain as a result of your thoughts. Bad feelings and attitudes arise from this process too.

That's because some of the chemicals that are triggered by our thoughts are "feel-good" chemicals; others are "downers."

How Your Thoughts Shape Your Character

You may wonder, aside from affecting our moods, does it really matter what we think? We're just talking about harmless thoughts, right?

Wrong. The truth is, the content of your thoughts matters a lot. You see, our thoughts can limit who we are and what we become, or they can act as the catalyst prompting us forward in our lives.

Our thoughts influence our character, shape our attitudes, determine our behaviors, affect our spirituality, and even influence the immune system, says author, educator, and psychologist Archibald Hart.[2] "Your thinking determines whether you will be happy or sad most of the time. It even determines if you'll get married and whether your sex life will be satisfying," he says.[3]

Let's assume this day isn't going so well for you. There have been frustrations and setbacks—other people not following through on commitments, loved ones not paying attention to your concerns, children misbehaving. You're feeling like Rhonda usually does, like nothing ever goes her way.

Now you have some angry, unkind, or cranky thoughts—and there's a consequence. Your brain releases chemicals that cause physical reactions. You may feel your muscles tense, your heart pound, your hands sweat. The body is a receptacle for every negative thought we have, and it reacts to each one.

Imagine the difference if you viewed your day as Melanie does, with a positive take on whatever comes your way. You'd skip all the unpleasant emotions and physical reactions that accompany negative thinking.

Your Thoughts and Your Health

Thoughts can create stress in our life. And it's been well documented that stress negatively affects health in many ways.

Humor, on the other hand, helps your brain function in a healthy way. In reacting to humor, both sides of the brain are activated simultaneously. When you tell a joke, the left side—the part responsible for thinking—starts firing. When you "get" a joke and start laughing, your right side becomes active.

Research indicates that people tend to be more creative when they see something as funny. Other studies suggest that laughter helps increase the flexibility and creativity of thinking. Humor even has been used to help strengthen the immune system.[4]

Thoughts create emotions that can have a lasting physical effect on your body. For example, when we dwell on old hurts and wounds, we build a mental habit. Every time we think about that pain from the past, stress—and its toxic effects—surfaces with increasing speed. Each time we think that negative thought, we build a stronger pathway to that negative emotion, and we're more likely to express ourselves in a negative way.

Our emotional pain can even trigger physical pain or damage. Researchers have linked toxic thoughts to heart and vascular problems, gastrointestinal problems, headaches, skin conditions, intestinal tract disorders, chronic pain, lung and breathing disorders, and immune impairment.[5]

Consider this, from Dr. Caroline Leaf's *Who Switched Off My Brain?*:

> Research shows that around 87% of illnesses can be attributed to our thought life, and approximately 13% to diet, genetics and environment. Studies conclusively link more chronic diseases (also known as lifestyle diseases) to

an epidemic of toxic emotions in our culture. These toxic emotions can cause migraines, hypertension, strokes, cancer, skin problems, diabetes, infections and allergies, just to name a few.[6]

As a negative thought begins to develop, it activates a section of the brain that releases emotions related to the thought. If it's a negative—or toxic—thought, one of those insidious "downer" chemicals is released, stimulating the release of another, which stimulates the release of yet another.

Chemicals released by negative emotions can affect your brain's nerve cells, causing difficulty in retrieving memories. That, in turn, suppresses the ability to remember and think in a constructive way. Chemicals released in the brain as a result of positive thoughts don't cause this kind of damage, research shows.

Toxic thoughts impact both emotional and physical balance. The hormones released can disrupt positive brain functioning,[7] making it difficult for us to concentrate or focus.

The good news is that our thoughts also can create a calmness that helps control our emotions, reining them in before they spin out of control. Every positive or happy thought spurs your brain to action, releasing chemicals that make your body feel good.

Why Self-Talk Matters

This is where the power of self-talk is so evident. Self-talk is simply the thoughts you tell yourself. For example, Melanie may step out of the house, notice it's raining, and think,

"Great, the yard needed some water." On the other hand, her friend Rhonda, who feeds herself a steady diet of negative self-talk, would probably think, "Oh, rats! Now I'll get my hair and shoes wet. And it will be rough driving in to work. And I'll probably catch a cold. And . . ." You get the picture.

Thoughts follow specific pathways in the brain. When a thought occurs, the part of the brain called the thalamus goes to work making sense of the information and running it through the part of the brain that stores memories, the amygdala. In her book, Dr. Leaf notes:

> Remember that the amygdala is much like a library and is responsible for the first emotional response to any thought. It activates and arouses you to do something. If your "library" is filled with "books" that tell a story about not being able to cope with the incoming information, the response will be to react to the information based purely on an emotional level. This is why it is never wise to react to the first emotion you feel. It is a physiological response designed to alert and focus you, not to direct your actions.[8]

When your thoughts are toxic or negative, you've handed off control to your emotions, chemical reactions that aren't always reliable. Part of the amygdala's purpose is to alert us. But unless it's steadied with nontoxic, balanced thoughts, the emotions it generates can dominate.[9] And that can cause a negative, even irrational, response.

That's why memories, even those we don't consciously recall, can have powerful effects. Even if they're not readily accessed by the brain, so-called hidden memories still exist. Their information isn't lost; it's stored somewhere in the mind. It's as if those memories are burned onto the hard drive of the mind, and when we hit the right keys to trigger them, they reappear clearly to us.

We all have memories hidden somewhere beyond our conscious memory, blocked because the event was extremely painful or traumatic. It's as though God has built into the functioning of our mind the ability to repress emotionally painful material. Some of these memories stay there until our subconscious minds believe it's "safe" to access them.

We need to remember that, like so many other things, accessing memories is a biological process.

Which memories did you activate today? Were they negative or positive? Did they hinder your life or enhance it?

We Are What We Think

You *can* learn to control your thoughts that change your brain's chemistry, affect your emotions, and even influence your character.

And that means you can have signficant control over your physical well-being too.

Pastor and author Charles Swindoll describes the power we have to direct our thoughts:

Thoughts, positive or negative, grow stronger together when fertilized with constant repetition. That may explain why so many who are gloomy and gray stay in that mood, and why others who are cheery and enthusiastic continue to be so, even in the midst of difficult circumstances. Please do not misunderstand. Happiness (like winning) is a matter of right thinking, not intelligence, age or position. Our performance is directly related to the thoughts we deposit in our memory bank. We can only draw on what we deposit.

What kind of performance would your car deliver if every morning before you left for work you scooped up a handful of dirt and put it in your crankcase? The fine tuned engine would soon be coughing and sputtering. Ultimately, it would refuse to start. The same is true of your life. Thoughts about yourself and attitudes toward others that are narrow, destructive and abrasive produce wear and tear on your mental motor. They send you off the road while others drive past.[10]

Stop for a moment and reflect on your thought life. What type of deposits do you usually make?

Science simply confirms what Scripture has been saying all along: We are shaped, in large part, by our thoughts. Why else would the great apostle Paul say, "Fix your thoughts on what is true and good and right" (Phil. 4:8 TLB)?

The Scriptures have much more to say about the act of thinking and our thought life. The words *think*, *thought*, and *mind* are used hundreds of times in the Bible. The writer of Proverbs 23:7 states succinctly: "As he thinks within himself, so he is" (NASB). Often the Scriptures refer to the heart as the source of our thoughts:

> The heart of the righteous weighs its answers,
> but the mouth of the wicked gushes evil.
>   (Prov. 15:28 NIV)

But the things that come out of the mouth come from the heart, and these make a man "unclean." For out of the heart come evil thoughts, murder, adultery, sexual immorality, theft, false testimony, slander. (Matt. 15:18–19 NIV)

God, of course, knows the content of our thoughts:

All the ways of a man are pure in his own eyes, but the Lord
weighs the spirits (the thoughts and intents of the heart).
(Prov. 16:2 AMP)

Our Creator designed us so that our thoughts have an
impact on every aspect of life. Positive thoughts bring about
positive effects. Negative thoughts take everything—from
attitude to health—in the opposite direction. No wonder
the author of Proverbs wrote,

> A cheerful heart is good medicine,
>   but a crushed spirit dries up the bones.
>   (Prov. 17:22 NIV)

He knew what modern science has confirmed: Negative
thoughts are a form of pollution to our body. What's more,
our thoughts—good and bad—affect what we say and do.
Jesus said,

The good man brings good things out of the good stored
up in his heart, and the evil man brings evil things out of
the evil stored up in his heart. For out of the overflow of
his heart his mouth speaks. (Luke 6:45 NIV)

Are your thoughts shaping you? Or are you shaping your
thoughts? And what are your thoughts producing?

If you're not in control of your mind, who *is*? Who has
control of what you think? You, or God? Think about this.

Clearly, our thoughts feed our emotions, and our emotions affect our health. So you know you must beware of

negative self-talk—it's toxic. But we aren't helpless victims of our thoughts. We can choose how they affect us. We simply must learn how to direct their course.

Taking Control

"I wish my mind wasn't so scattered."

"My mind feels so divided."

"My thoughts are so fragmented."

I've asked people who make these statements, "Is that the first time you've said that?" They look at me like I've lost my senses. Usually, they confess that those statements have been constant companions. No wonder they feel this way!

When we repeat any statement enough, even unintentionally, we can cause it, over time, to become reality. Again, let's think about Rhonda. When she repeats to herself over and over that she's probably going to have a bad day—guess what? She experiences so many negative emotions—and even significant physiological reactions, such as upset stomach, headache, or nervousness—that other problems occur, and simply as a result of her negative self-talk, she does, indeed, have a bad day.

Now, it's all right to repeat statements. In fact, we're going to repeat many of them the rest of our lives.

But we need to beware of negative statements, especially about our own minds. We don't have to feel scattered, divided, and fragmented. We've been given more than that as believers.

The Bible promises the believer a sound, well-balanced mind. In 2 Timothy, Paul writes, "For God did not give us a spirit of timidity (of cowardice, of craven and cringing and fawning fear), but [He has given us a spirit] of power and of love and of calm *and* well-balanced mind *and* discipline *and* self-control" (1:7 AMP, emphasis added).

Scriptural teaching about our thoughts is not just informative; it's encouraging—and potentially life changing. Memorizing and dwelling upon this Scripture can help bring order to your thought life and, as a result, improve your relationships, health, and happiness.

Imagine the impact if we countered every thought about being scattered, divided, and fragmented with this forceful self-talk: "Stop—that's not true!"

Imagine the power of repeating the encouraging passage from 2 Timothy 1:7 aloud. This can become a self-fulfilling prophecy too. And the result? A person who is calm, disciplined, and self-controlled, with a well-balanced mind, can create more of this positive, self-fulfilling prophecy.

So yes, you really can:

Think yourself healthy.

Think yourself successful.

Think yourself out of worry and anxiety.

Think yourself out of bitterness and resentment.

Think yourself into forgiving.

Think yourself in control of your emotions.

Think yourself out of stress.

Think yourself happy.

The possibilities are limitless!

Some people say they feel they're responsible *to* their mind. The problem with that is we've given control to whatever is raging. When we give our mind control, we think we have to go along with whatever upset, worry, anxiety, or depressive thought might be occurring. Being responsible to it means going along with whatever's occurring.

You can learn to be responsible *for* your mind. And that's essentially what Scripture instructs us to do. We can learn to direct our mind to reflect God's will. And because experiencing emotions based on thinking this way is a biochemical event, following scriptural principles creates a different biochemical solution, the kind that God desires for us. Clearly, it's a better way to live.

Your thoughts—and their biochemical reactions—shape your emotional and physical health. I repeat this for a reason—so you'll be conscious of this as you go about your daily life. It's a new thought that can impact your life in a new way.

New thoughts or old memories—both can direct your life. It's possible to change and control them. In this book, you'll learn how.

Reflect and Remember

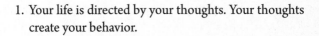

1. Your life is directed by your thoughts. Your thoughts create your behavior.

2. Your thoughts affect the chemistry in your brain.

3. Your thoughts and your emotions are closely linked. Toxic thoughts create negative emotions.

4. You can learn to be responsible for your mind. We are what we think.

5. God knows our thoughts. God gives us a well-balanced mind.

6. What happened in your life today because of what you thought?

_____

_____

_____

_____

2

Where Do Thoughts Come From?

Stephanie is beginning to worry about the thoughts that pop into her mind from seemingly out of nowhere. Why can't I focus? she wonders.

Sometimes when talking to a friend, she'll suddenly realize that, on the outside, she looks like she's really into the conversation and really listening, but on the inside, she's drifting, analyzing her friend's words. She catches herself only pretending to be paying attention.

When driving, sometimes, she catches herself imagining her life as an outsider watching a heroine in a full-scale Hollywood movie production. She "sees" herself in high-action adventure, as her mind races along, taking her with it for the ride. Now and then, the image of a scary accident—twisted metal, ambulances, wounded people—pops into her mind. Her body tenses and her heart pounds.

At other times, she inadvertently starts recalling her most recent conversation with her mother, in all its full detail, complete with the mix of frustration and guilt that was triggered by it.

And she's been alarmed recently when the image of a male co-worker has popped into her mind. *I don't mean to think about him in a romantic way!* she worries. *So why do I find myself imagining a romantic fantasy world with him? I love my husband, and I don't want anyone else!*

It's like my mind never turns off! she frets, recalling a magazine article that claimed women's minds are always "on." *Do men have this problem? Because it sure seems like my husband's comes on when it needs to, and then turns off until he needs it again!*

Why do I have all these thoughts? she wonders. *It's like someone else put them into my mind. I don't want to take responsibility for some of them—that's for sure! Isn't there any way to get my mind back on track . . . and keep it there?*

The Source of Our Thoughts

Thoughts come and go. But from where? Do we always "think" them? Do we choose them? Are they based in what we believe to be true? Or are they truly random?

We already know that thoughts affect our feelings and body. But we have to remember: Our thoughts may or may not reflect reality.

It's common to wonder, as Stephanie frequently does, Am I responsible for all the thoughts I think? For the answer, we can look at Scripture.

We can have great intentions to follow this directive: "Set your minds and keep them set on what is above (the higher things), not on the things that are on the earth" (Col. 3:2 AMP). But even when we're trying to do that, we have those other not-so-good, not-so-healthy, not-so-Christian thoughts that flash on the screens of our minds. We didn't want them. We didn't invite them. They just showed up.

In most cases, we can't stop specific thoughts from coming to mind. Our task is to manage them once they arrive.

It's like the different individuals who come to your door. Some might walk right in without being invited. Do you invite them to stay? I doubt it. You evict them.

Once unwelcome thoughts pop in, you have the choice to either allow them to stay or kick them out. That's where your responsibility lies. Think about it: What does the word *set* mean to you in the verse from Colossians?

Thoughts about recent trauma, or even trauma from far in the past, all the way back to childhood, also may flash through your mind.

Vivid dreams or nightmares, as well as thoughts, may take up residence in your mind. You feel as if you're reliving the event over again. The experience seems embedded or tattooed on your brain.

It's like the crash scene Stephanie sometimes imagines as she drives. She probably saw a crash like that as a child. It made an impression on her then. And even though she is no longer aware of the memory, her brain has never "let it go."

Scientists aren't sure why thoughts like these come to mind. But they have confirmed differences between the brains of men and women. Stephanie's right in sensing that her brain is always "on," even though it seems her husband's brain switches off when he's not specifically thinking about something. Research using brain scans has shown that a woman's brain really is "on" all the time, whereas a man's brain "turns on" when he uses it, and "turns off" when he's no longer thinking about something purposefully.[1]

> Bottom line: We need to kick out unwelcome, uninvited, negative thoughts, and "set our minds," as Scripture instructs, on thoughts that are good, healthful, uplifting, and positive.

Bottom line: We need to kick out unwelcome, uninvited, negative thoughts, and "set our minds," as Scripture instructs, on thoughts that are good, healthful, uplifting, and positive.

I look at it like this: Every now and then, a strange animal wanders into my yard. I didn't invite it. And if it shows potential to do harm, I must engage in damage control *before* it affects me or my property.

We need to treat our thoughts with the same urgency.

Automatic Thoughts and How They Affect Us

Many of our thoughts are automatic. We don't intentionally think them. We might even rather not think them.

They can be positive or negative. But they jump into our consciousness without any planning or conscious prompting. And they often carry a specific message.

For example, a young woman who's afraid of being rejected by men frequently tells herself, after meeting an interesting young man: He isn't interested in me. I'm not attractive enough.

By repeating this thought to herself over and over, she reinforces her belief in it—whether it's true or not. She doesn't intend to think it. It just pops into her mind when she considers her romantic possibilities. It has become automatic.

Often, an automatic thought surfaces, not in complete form, but in a shorthand manner. It may take the form of a visual image or just a few words, such as a brief memory or a series of disconnected words, that brings to mind an entire group of painful memories, fears, or self-degrading comments.

Though these thoughts appear spontaneously, we tend to think of them as true. The thought is *there*, we rationalize. Why *shouldn't* it be true?

But when we fail to test toxic thoughts, comparing them to what we know is true, they can begin to occur more frequently—and we believe them more and more.

Automatic thoughts often include the words *must, should,* or *ought.* These are "torture words," because they elevate guilt and lower self-esteem.

"I should do this . . ." or "I must be a perfect mother" or "I ought to be consistent and never make a mistake."

When these words appear on the screen of your mind, they generate hopelessness. We'll hear more about these words later in this book.

Automatic thoughts "awfulize" situations. These thoughts expect the worst, see the danger behind every bush, and create intense anxiety—and they often appear somewhat reasonable.

They can color our attitude for days. And because they just pop in, they may be camouflaged amid other thoughts. It's hard to put a leash on them, as they tend to come and go. Have you ever tried to put a leash on a dog that's moving around? It just doesn't happen.

Automatic thoughts are learned. We listen to others and what they say about us, and we believe the statements. And what's more, we tend to become what we believe.

Giving God Control

Many of our thoughts are more than just thoughts. They're rigid beliefs, things we believe to be absolute truth. Often they're negative. Often they're untrue. Yet we believe them wholeheartedly.

Rigid beliefs are a form of self-imprisonment. Your mind uses them to put you under a kind of house arrest. You may think they're helping you, but the truth is they exclude you from discovering the truth, something better.[2]

We've always had this struggle with our thoughts. It began with the fall of man.

Isn't it interesting that the first place human beings turned away from God was in our thoughts? Genesis 6:5 says, "Then the LORD saw that the wickedness of man was great on the earth, and that every intent of the thoughts of his heart was only evil continually" (NASB).

> While we can't always choose our thoughts, we do have freedom to choose on which thoughts we dwell.

It's also in our thoughts that we need to turn our lives back toward him. While we can't always choose our thoughts, we do have freedom to choose on which thoughts we dwell. But because we're "dead in trespasses and sins," according to Ephesians 2:1 (KJV), we can't simply determine to banish all toxic thinking, unless God is involved in the process.[3]

So when uninvited, unplanned thoughts pop in, we can learn to automatically evaluate them, asking ourselves, Does this thought contradict the teaching of the Word of God? And we can ask the Holy Spirit for guidance.

The solution isn't to try to control the content of your mind on your own. Instead, choose to give God the control. Romans 8:5–7 warns,

> Those who live according to the sinful nature have their minds set on what that nature desires; but those who live in accordance with the Spirit have their minds set on what the Spirit desires. The mind of sinful man is death, but the

mind controlled by the Spirit is life and peace; the sinful mind is hostile to God. It does not submit to God's law, nor can it do so. (NIV)

Our goal should be to let our mind be controlled by the Spirit. We should want to set it on what God wants. We'll learn specific ways to do that in later chapters.

At night, I like to go to sleep listening to the music of a particular radio station. It's a bit tricky to tune in and get the right one. A fraction of a move to the left or the right and I'll miss it, so I have to work at setting it just right. It's the same with our mind.

We have to make sure we have it set just right on what is good and positive.

Identifying Destructive Patterns in *Your* Thinking

Remember Stephanie? Her thoughts about her co-worker were both automatic and destructive. But she can break the cycle by asking herself these questions when she catches herself thinking in that way:

- What was going through my mind just before I started to feel this way?
- What does this say about me, if it's true?
- What does this mean about me, my life, my future?
- What am I afraid might happen?
- What is the worst thing that could happen, if this is true?
- What does this mean about how the other person(s) feel(s)/think(s) about me?

- What does this mean about the other person(s) or people in general?
- What images or memories do I have in this situation?[4]

By doing this, Stephanie can steal the power from her automatic thoughts. The result is more balanced thinking and freedom from stress.

Becoming aware of our automatic thoughts—our self-talk—is a necessary step in the journey toward change. Just identifying the ten to fifteen most common phrases we say to ourselves is a good beginning. Then we can disarm those negative thoughts.

What do you tell yourself frequently? That you're always stressed? Always late? Always forgetting things? That you should be more organized? More disciplined? More patient?

You might not even be aware of the automatic thoughts that damage your perception of yourself. You can start identifying them by challenging negative thoughts and purposefully putting them through the verification process, as Stephanie did.

When you begin to recognize them, and realize how frequently they pass through your mind, you may be shocked. When they begin to identify their negative self-talk, people frequently say, "I can't believe what I've been saying to myself for all these years!"

Just imagine how many thousands of times you may have made these automatic, negative statements to yourself. Now consider this: This self-talk sets the course for how you're to live your life. With every one of these automatic thoughts, you're actually giving yourself directions.

If the context of your self-talk is negative or toxic, what's the result? Well, you could end up immobilized, fearful, insecure, stuck, negative toward yourself and others, and just plain miserable.

Reversing the Engines

Here's the good news: Any negative self-talk phrase can be reversed. It can be reframed as a realistic, positive statement. Like a boat that's been moving in the wrong direction, you can turn your self-talk around and start moving your thoughts—and your life—in another direction.

So when a negative thought occurs, consider the eight questions Stephanie addressed, and answer them for yourself. What did you learn?

Have you struggled to change your thought life? Of course you have. We all have. Maybe you've tried different approaches or programs, prayed about it, been prayed over, and so on. But you still struggle.

Any change you want to make is not a simple step-by-step process or an overnight event. That's because your brain wasn't designed to make sudden and permanent changes.

The brain follows patterns of habits established over the years. We can't expect this unique organ of the body—with its billions of neurons and millions of pathways, circuits, and memory cells—to erase what it's built over years, replacing it with entirely new thinking instantaneously.

When we try to make sudden changes, we ask the brain to do something it wasn't designed to do. So when we begin changing old patterns, we should expect old ways of thinking and talking to challenge the new. We're likely to tell ourselves things like, This won't work. You can't believe these new thoughts.

But this is good! It shows the new approach is working. You've disrupted that old way of thinking, and now it's resisting the change.

It's similar to the struggle we have in living the Christian life. When we put on our new self, our old sinful self rears its head. A battle between the two emerges.

Because so much of what we do and say stems from our self-talk, we have to expect some tension and conflict when we start doing something new.

For change to occur, and it can, we need to make changes in a way that fits into the brain's normal operation.[5] And the Bible warns that it's a process we must take seriously. Consider Matthew 12:43–45:

> When an evil spirit comes out of a man, it goes through arid places seeking rest and does not find it. Then it says, "I will return to the house I left." When it arrives, it finds the house unoccupied, swept clean and put in order. Then it goes and takes with it seven other spirits more wicked than itself, and they go in and live there. And the final condition of that man is worse than the first. That is how it will be with this wicked generation. (NIV)

Think about the place where you have all of your thoughts as your house. It's furnished throughout with everything you think about yourself and the world. Many of the furnishings were handed down to you by others.

This furniture includes the toxic or negative self-talk you inherited from parents, friends, siblings, teachers, and others.

These individuals gave you your furnishings, and you've held on to them for years, continuing to use them. Some of this tattered, hand-me-down furniture sags with wear and threatens to collapse.

Now, a friend has agreed to help you get rid of the junk. He's going to help you eliminate negative thinking patterns permanently. They'll be gone for good. So the two of you meet and begin boxing everything up, carrying every single item out of the house and into the garage. Rugs, stove, beds, tables, chairs—everything's on its way out. Every old self-belief now is stored in the garage, where no one can see it.

When your friend leaves, you go back inside the house. It looks so much larger without any furnishings. It's empty. It's clean. It smells better.

> If you simply try to empty your mind of negative thoughts, but fail to replace them with positive thoughts, the negative thoughts will return.

There's not one negative thought available. You begin to think, Now I'll have positive thoughts! I'll be a positive thinker!

There you are—alone with your big, empty "house." You wander from room to room. You like it, now that you've removed all those old, worn, negative thoughts.

But your house feels so empty. An hour goes by. Two. Three. You're thinking, This is great! I've evicted all my old negative thoughts. There's not one in sight!

But the emptiness gets to you. So after a while, you decide to revisit the old stuff. You go out to the garage. You see an item that feels so familiar. It's this old negative thought: I don't have much to offer in a relationship.

You think, This won't hurt anything. I'll just take this one item back.

A bit later, you repeat the process. And over the next few hours, you retrieve it all. Why? You're comfortable with all those thoughts, bad as they are. You're used to them.

We have difficulty with a void or vacuum in our mind. If you simply try to empty your mind of negative thoughts, but fail to replace them with positive thoughts, the negative thoughts will return.

When you clean out your "house," it's more productive to discard or destroy the old furniture, rather than store it, keeping it available.

You'll be more successful bringing in a load of new "furniture"—positive, healthy thoughts and self-talk.

Keeping the Forward Momentum

Remember, though, your brain is used to the old thoughts. What it needs is constant detail from you. Specific directions, words, results, and directives are what your brain needs[6] as it learns a new way of thinking, new self-talk.

Your goal is to learn to regard your thoughts as you might watch clouds floating by. Mental events float past, and you see them for what they are—thoughts, and not necessarily reality.

Stephanie confesses, "Sometimes I feel as though I've been kidnapped by my thoughts. Twenty minutes later I seem to come out of this fog or inner trance and come back to reality. It's like I missed out on twenty minutes of my life!"

She's not alone. Some people often feel as if they've been swept away by a thought flood. It's as though you went to the movies, and your mind got out of its seat and was drawn into the action on the screen, and it's now a participant, rather than an observer. It's like you've been drawn into believing your thoughts are reality.

When your thoughts feel like reality, your mind is swept away. It's like hopping onto a train without realizing it. Eventually, you realize you've snoozed through a ride. When you step off the train, you will be at a much different place than where you jumped on.[7]

It may be helpful to give your toxic self-talk a name, and then use that name when you recognize those thoughts. You might call them Pollution Words, Hopeless Words, The Critic, The Enemy, Satan's Agent, The Liar. When we use a label like one of these, it helps us see these thoughts as occasional visitors, rather than permanent residents. It helps us remember that these visiting enemies don't represent who we really are.

Consider what Peter McWilliams writes in *You Can't Afford the Luxury of a Negative Thought*:

> For many, negative thinking is a habit, which, over time, becomes an addiction. It's a disease, like alcoholism, compulsive overeating, or drug abuse.
>
> A lot of people suffer from this disease because negative thinking is addictive to each of The Big Three—the mind, the body and the emotions. If one doesn't get you, the others are waiting in the wings.

The mind becomes addicted to being "right." In this far-less-than-perfect world, one of the easiest ways to be right is to predict failure—especially for ourselves. The mind likes being right. When asked, "Would you rather be right or be happy?" some people—who really take the time to consider the ramifications of being "wrong"—have trouble deciding.

The body becomes addicted to the rush of chemicals poured into the blood stream by the Fight or Flight Response. Some people can't resist the physical stimulation of a serious session of negative thinking. They get off on the rush of adrenalin.

The emotions become addicted to the sheer intensity of it all. The Fight or Flight Response may not trigger pleasant feelings, but at least they're not boring. As the emotions become accustomed to a higher level of stimulation, they begin demanding more and more intensity. It's not unlike the slash-and-gash movies—too much is no longer enough.[8]

Dan had struggled with his thoughts for years, and discovered that putting a label on them was a breakthrough. He said, "When I was able to create a label that summarized my thought theme, I also began to label the intrusion of these thoughts as visits. My thoughts were an uninvited, unwelcomed visitor. I saw it as one of those unnecessary visits, and began to challenge my negative thoughts with, 'Oh, it's you again. Oh well, you've pretty well worn out your welcome and any usefulness that you may have had. There's no real use for you to stick around anymore. I've got better thoughts now.' I know it sounds crazy to carry on this kind of conversation with my thoughts, but it works for me."

Whenever you have a toxic or negative thought, do a little digging. Investigate. Acknowledge the pressure of your visitor with its name or label. Talk to it. "Here you are again."

The authors of *The Mindful Way through Depression* suggest this technique for zapping the power of negative thoughts:

> Identifying and naming our recurrent thought patterns is one way to help us see the "tapes in the mind" for what they are. Recognizing them when they are starting up allows us to say: "Ah, I know this tape; this is my 'I'm a total failure' tape or my 'I'll never be happy' tape." This will not necessarily switch it off, or if it appears to, it will almost certainly return soon. The difference will be in the way we relate to it: as a fact that we can do little about, or as a highly conditioned and inaccurate "tape" running in the mind that will continue to be an inconvenience until the "batteries" run down and it ceases of its own accord.[9]

Remember: Don't accept every thought as a fact. Begin to challenge each one.

When you engage in challenging your thoughts— questioning their source and whether they're even true— that process allows your brain to create new responses and sift the information. But for this to be really effective, there is only one way to do it—out loud.

That's right, you need to speak the words. It enhances your ability to think on a higher level. Hearing your own voice aloud has greater impact on your brain than just saying the words to yourself silently.

To control your thoughts, you must identify them and challenge them in this way. Toxic thoughts aren't neutral.

They're in the construction business. They build toxic memories. And when you file a toxic memory away in your memory bank, it generates toxic emotions and thoughts whenever you revisit it.

New thoughts create new pathways in your brain. These add to the abundance of stored memories. They expand your functioning. You choose whether they'll affect you for better . . . or for worse.

Test the reality of your thoughts by saying them out loud (in private, of course). It makes you more aware of the abundance of the thoughts you have about yourself or others. And it makes you more aware of their content.

When you actually hear your thoughts spoken aloud, you're more likely to evaluate them better. You may respond, "That really is true!" Or you may object, "That's so far from the truth it's ridiculous!"

Your sense of hearing can help you evaluate false, negative self-talk for what it is . . . untruth. Then you can talk back—with truth!

> When you actually hear your thoughts spoken aloud, you're more likely to evaluate them better.

Eventually, Stephanie learned to fight off those romantic thoughts about another man—thoughts she didn't want to be having—by listing the positive qualities of her husband and all the things she really did love about him. She did this out loud. And the more she did it, the more she focused on her husband. The worrisome thoughts about her co-worker faded away.

This process has been called "voice therapy." It was developed to help bring toxic or negative thoughts to the surface, along with any emotions connected to them.

With practice, the process will feel more natural. It may also help to speak the self-talk in second person, instead of in first person. For example, instead of saying, "I'm so unattractive," you'd say, "You're so unattractive."

Saying it in this way may help identify where the thought originated. Was the source a sibling? A "friend"? A parent?[10]

If you've buried the source, unearthing it in this way can help you challenge the statement and identify it as false. By doing so, you tear down the negative effects of that self-talk, eventually redirecting it in a positive direction. There is hope!

Reflect and Remember

1. What's the greatest source for your thoughts?

   _____

   _____

2. What label will you use to describe your recurring negative thoughts?

   _____

   _____

3. What's the plan that you'll use to challenge your thoughts? Describe your challenge.

   _____

   _____

4. In what way do your thoughts reflect the Word of God?

   _____

   _____

The Gift of Imagination

Janice and Sue giggled their way through school together, acting out vivid story lines in their imaginary play at recess and after dismissal. Teachers complained they shared an overactive fantasy life.

As they grew into adulthood, the friends still used their creative thoughts. For Janice, it paid off in a career in advertising. What she concocted in her mind propelled her to the top of her profession. Colleagues raved, "Where do you come up with such off-the-wall ideas? They're great!"

Sue still nursed an active imagination too. But hers didn't seem to make life better. For her, imagined thoughts increasingly became a source of discord in relationships. She would rehearse encounters with others, then analyze them afterward, dwelling, most often, on any negative possibilities.

Both Janice and Sue were affecting their lives with their imaginations . . . but with very different results.

Daydreams, Fantasies, and Imagination

In *Eleonora*, Edgar Allan Poe wrote, "They who dream by day are cognizant of many things which escape those who dream only by night."[1] And surely that's true. Daydreams can help us harness our creativity, reach our full potential.

Do you dream by day? I do. In fact, some days, I do it a lot, especially when I'm in the process of crafting a book. Or as I prepare for a presentation, I go over the material in my mind, adding ideas as they come to me. Or as I anticipate a vacation or an encounter with someone, I imagine what might happen.

God gave us this wonderful gift—a twofold ability to see. We can visually observe what goes on around us. We also can "see" pictures in our minds. The latter ability, especially, can help us achieve wonderful things, as in Janice's case. Or, that same imagination can hold us back, when we use it in a negative way, like Sue.

Our imaginations are busy with pictures and ideas all day long. It's too bad we don't have a device that's able to record and recall all of these "pictures," and track the time we spend on them. On second thought . . . perhaps it's best we don't.

There are times when we retreat into the safety of our daydreams when our real world isn't pleasant. Children do this when they live in a hostile or unsafe environment.

But there are differences between imagination, daydreaming, and fantasy. Imagination is a creation of the mind, the ability to form a mental image. Daydreaming is usually a wishful creation of the mind. Fantasy is using the imagination to create mental images that are often unrealistic.

When our real life is drab or boring or unfulfilled, we may slip into the recesses of our thought life for satisfaction. Unfortunately, this can become such a convenient escape that we begin to choose it over real life. And then we may fail to make real changes that would make life more fulfilling.

For example, a man may envision himself moving up in his company. In his mind, he enjoys that "success." But he fails to participate in training seminars, read books that could help him improve his skills, or attend company classes that could help him truly achieve that success that fills his daydreams.

And many a marriage relationship has been fractured because the husband chose to live in a world of sexual fantasies fed by pornography, rather than focus on his wife and the real world.

> God gave us this wonderful gift—a twofold ability to see. We can visually observe what goes on around us. We also can "see" pictures in our minds.

Imagery at Work

So what comes to your mind when the word *imagery* is mentioned? Do you think using imagery is some mysterious practice? Or is it a gift from God to be used in a positive way?

Imagery is simply the forming of mental pictures or images.

The imagery of fantasy and daydreams is a characteristic of human life. Our ability to imagine sets us apart from animals.

Christian writer and pastor A. W. Tozer describes imagination in this way:

> Like every other power belonging to us, the imagination may be either a blessing or a curse, depending altogether upon how it is used and how well it is disciplined.
>
> We all have to some degree the power to imagine. This gift enables us to see meanings in material objects, to observe similarities between things which at first appear wholly unlike each other. It permits us to know that which the sense can never tell us, for by it we are able to see through sense impressions to the reality that lies behind things.
>
> Every advance made by mankind in any field began as an idea to which nothing for the time corresponded. The mind of the inventor took bits of familiar ideas and made out of them something altogether nonexistent. Thus we "create" things and by so doing prove ourselves to have been made in the image of the Creator.[2]

Daydreams have been responsible for some of our greatest discoveries and human creations. Thomas Edison didn't just sit down and invent the lightbulb. He first lay on the couch in his workshop and filled his mind with fantasies about lightbulbs and electricity. French composer Claude Debussy created some of his music by viewing reflections of the sun on the river.

Every great cathedral once existed only as an idea in someone's mind. That imagery was translated into magnificent reality.

Fantasy can rescue us from drudgery or lead us in the creation of a masterpiece—the former serves as an escape, the latter leads to accomplishment. Fantasy can also

> Daydreams have been responsible for some of our greatest discoveries and human creations.

be used to help heal our negative and toxic memories and free us from self-condemnation, when used in a positive and realistic way.

It can be used as a powerful magnet to draw out our strengths and abilities, to unlock problems, and to tear down barriers blocking progress and growth.

Athletes often claim that mental imagery is about 50 percent of their game. Ballplayers often imagine where they want the ball to finish, and then imagine the trajectory and shape of the ball during the shot.

The key is to ensure you're using your imagination in a positive way.

What images are in your mind today? What are their purposes, and how are you using them? Do you have any that seem to get stuck in your mind, and no matter how hard you try you can't get rid of them?

In Genesis 6:5 the word *imagination* is used for the first time: "The Lord saw that the wickedness of man was great in the earth, and that every imagination and intention of all human thinking was only evil continually" (AMP). So even from the beginning of time, we see one of God's greatest gifts misused and distorted. Not only that, the word *continually* shows us that people's evil thoughts were, in effect, "stuck" in their minds. And it started when they were young, according to Genesis 8:21: "For the imagination . . . of man's heart is evil and wicked from his youth" (AMP).

This struggle begins early, and "sticks" with us, you might say.

Have you ever started the day irritated over something your spouse did or said to you? During the day you ruminated on it, visualizing what you were going to do and say when you next saw your spouse. Mentally, you practiced your delivery, time and time again. When your spouse made an appearance, you were ready with a well-rehearsed description of the offense . . . and your displeasure! He or she may have been amazed at the refinement of your presentation. In fact, it was worthy of an Oscar! But then, you'd prepared well. Imagine if you'd prepared in a positive manner.

The Power of Imagery

Imagery is actually the basis for our thought processes. It's a way we process information. As infants, the first words we learn are those connected to concrete images: Mama, dog, ball.

People who describe images with great detail and accuracy often become authors or storytellers. If you've ever listened to

"The Prairie Home Companion" radio show, you've probably heard host Garrison Keillor tell fascinating stories about the fictitious small town Lake Wobegon. As he expertly paints mental pictures with vivid details, the images and people he describes leap out from the radio. The listener feels like part of the action, all thanks to imagery.

Shakespeare and other authors employ tremendous range of vocabulary to help us to see, smell, hear, taste, and feel details in their stories. The clever use of words creates images in our minds. I enjoy reading westerns by Louis L'Amour because his writing turns the scenes into dust-kicking, gun-twirling, bronc-busting life in my mind.

Imaging is the forming of mental pictures or images. And interestingly, the way we imagine ourselves, we are likely to become.

If we imagine ourselves as failing, we're more likely to fail. If we imagine ourselves as succeeding in some task, there's a greater likelihood that we'll succeed. For example, it's been well documented that tennis players who mentally practice their game improve more than those who don't.

And images we believe and reinforce eventually seep into the unconscious part of our minds, becoming part of who we are.

Vincent Collins, author of *Me, Myself and You*, describes the process in this way: "Imagination is to the emotions what illustrations are to a text, what music is to a ballad. It is the ability to form mental pictures, to visualize irritating or fearful situations in concrete form. As soon as we perceive a feeling and begin to think about it, the imagination goes to work. The imagination reinforces the thoughts, the thoughts intensify the feelings, and the whole business builds up."[3]

Scottish preacher Alexander Whyte describes the power of imagination in Hannah Hurnard's *Winged Life*: "It makes us full of eyes, without and within. The imagination is far stronger than any other power which we possess, and the psychologists tell us that on occasions, when the will and the imagination are in conflict, the imagination always wins. How important therefore that we should vow by the Savior's help never to throw the wrong kind of pictures on this screen in our minds, for the imagination literally has the power of making the things we picture real and effective."[4]

So we must guard our imagination, remembering that it was damaged in the fall, and because of that, can be distorted and misused.

The apostle Paul writes, "Now this I affirm . . . that you must no longer live as the Gentiles do, in the *futility* of their minds" (Eph. 4:17 RSV, emphasis added). In Romans 1:21, he again makes reference to the negative aspects of the imagination: "They became *futile* . . . in their thinking . . . and their senseless minds were darkened" (AMP, emphasis added).

And the author of 1 Chronicles 28:9 writes, "And you, my son Solomon, acknowledge the God of your father, and serve him with wholehearted devotion and with a willing mind, for the LORD searches every heart and understands every motive behind the thoughts. If you seek him, he will be found by you; but if you forsake him, he will reject you forever" (NIV).

God understands our thoughts and our motives. And his instruction about our thoughts is clear: We are to serve God with total dedication and an open and willing mind. Remember, God knows what's behind every thought we have.

Depending on how it's used, imagination can be a blessing or a royal pain. It's like a giant movie screen, and all day long we throw various episodes on it. As in most films, someone has the leading role. Who has the leading role in your movies? Well, if you're like the rest of us, you do. You've cast yourself as the central figure. It's normal. But how do you see yourself? A hero or a villain? Positive or negative?

God's Desire for Your Mind

God designed and gave us our minds—a unique blessing to the pinnacle of his creation. He also gave us instructions on how to protect and use that precious gift.

He says in his Word (emphasis added):

- Love the Lord your God with all your heart, and with all your soul, and with all your *mind*, and with all your strength. (Mark 12:30 NASB; see also Matt. 22:37; Luke 10:27)
- Then He opened their *minds* to understand the Scriptures. (Luke 24:45 NASB)
- Those who live according to the sinful nature have their *minds* set on what that nature desires; but those who live in accordance with the Spirit have their *minds* set on what the Spirit desires. (Rom. 8:5 NIV)
- Do not conform any longer to the pattern of this world, but be transformed by the renewing of your *mind*. (Rom. 12:2 NIV)
- Whatever is true, whatever is noble, whatever is right, whatever is pure, whatever is lovely, whatever is admirable—if anything is excellent or praiseworthy—*think* about such things. (Phil. 4:8 NIV)[5]

Retraining Yourself to Use Your Imagination for Good

The mind is a unique and wonderful creation. With it we can solve problems and craft masterpieces. With it we can also create problems that don't even exist.

In the images that play in our minds, we may depict ourselves as a functioning hero, or as an ineffective loser. We make judgments about ourselves and others. And sometimes, we see these imagined events as reality.

Maybe, like Sue, you allow your imagination to have a negative effect on your life. You *can* turn that around.

We don't have to allow our imaginations to get the better of us. With practice, we can snatch away the power of toxic, negative imagined thoughts.

When it occurs, we can speak right to that self-talk spawned by imagination, saying, "You're not reality—you're a passing mental event!" As we assert that again and again, we can break the hold of the negative imagery we've allowed to root in our minds.

Dave Matthew, the author of *A Sound Mind*, suggests bringing your imagination, "with all its power to shape your future," under control by becoming the "film producer" of the mental cinema screen in your mind.[6]

Appear "as the person *God* declares you to be in his Word," Matthew suggests. "You can do it. In fact, you must—you're responsible, remember?"

Matthew asserts that God's Word declares you to be "an individual chosen in Christ Jesus before the creation of the world, a child of none less than God himself, and greatly loved, a person through whom the Holy Spirit works for the blessing of others, someone triumphant in all circumstances—the list could go on and on. Create imagination films that portray you in this positive, biblical way, and that is what you will increasingly become."[7]

That doesn't mean you won't find yourself watching reruns of the negative stuff you used to play in your mind. The enemy will try to switch projectors on you.

That's when you take charge, choosing instead to play the mental images that feed your mind and imagination—and mold your character—with the truths of God's Word.

Reflect and Remember

1. Of what do you often daydream? What are the negative consequences of that imagery?

   _____

   _____

2. What could you do to make your thinking less futile, as described in God's Word?

   _____

   _____

3. What does a willing mind mean to you?

   _____

   _____

4. What steps will you take to train your imagination?

   _____

   _____

4

Core Beliefs—The Source of Your Thoughts

Jim was a pretty successful guy . . . or so others thought. Good-looking, good job, great family, nice home. From all appearances, he had it made—at least it looked that way from the outside. But the struggles inside his head told a whole different story.

Negative messages played one after another throughout the day. One day, he opened up to his close friend Sam, revealing his problem. It was almost, Jim confessed, like he had a critic or an internal commentator inside of his head that kept making negative statements to him, in the midst of all his apparent successes. The problem was, he listened to these more than to the good things he was experiencing!

Jim admitted that most of the negative messages had come from his past—from parents and teachers who were long gone. But now, his own voice took the place of theirs.

Jim was frustrated. He wanted to stop the bombardment of negative messages about himself. But he didn't know how.

He was shocked when Sam revealed simply, "Me too!"

The Origin of Your Core Beliefs

"Where did that thought come from?"

If you're like I am, you've asked that question about thoughts that pop into your mind. And sometimes, we're not only surprised, but shocked.

By the time we're adults, we've constructed a fairly good-sized mental filing cabinet. It's filled with beliefs about ourselves, about others, about life and God—our core beliefs.

Core beliefs are the source of what we believe and how we feel about ourself. They come from many sources and provide the fuel for many of our thoughts. Your automatic thoughts are based on your core beliefs deep inside.

I'm sure if you've done any cooking, you've come face-to-face with a raw onion. To use the onion, you usually need to peel off layer after layer. We have similar layers in our mind. As they pile up, they intensify our beliefs about ourselves.

Our core beliefs have been shaped since childhood by a vast array of family relationships, family patterns, and family rules and influence. Those play a major role in our thought life.

Your family instilled in you a pattern of thought as expressions and behaviors. You may have heard frequently, "You can't trust anyone," or "You should expect to be disappointed by other people."

Some thought patterns are positive; some aren't. Some are like seeds, which may lie dormant for years, then suddenly spring into life.

When you were growing up, did you have perfect parents? I doubt it. All of us are flawed, some worse than others.

Have you ever wondered what your grandparents and your parents talked about in their own minds? Wouldn't it be amazing if we'd had a device to give us a peek!

What do you think their self-talk was like? Was it healthy and positive, or negative and self-defeating? What they said to you and how they behaved toward you provide clues to the content of their own self-talk. If they're still alive, you might ask.

Is this really important? Extremely! You see, what they said to themselves with all their own personal distortions and limitations helped to shape your own life, as well as your self-talk.

> Research indicates that as much as 75 percent of everything we think is negative, counter-productive, and works against us.

Many of us were raised with negative programming. Consider this question: By the time you were eighteen years old,

63

how many times did you hear the word *no*? Several hundred? More than 50,000 times?

If you were raised in a fairly average, reasonably positive environment, it could have been more than 100,000 times. During the same period, how often do you think you were told what you *could do* or could accomplish in life? Thousands of times? Hundreds? Many can't remember more than a few. For most individuals, the *yes* statements didn't balance out the *nos*.

Research indicates that as much as 75 percent of everything we think is negative, counterproductive, and works against us. Most of what we have been influenced by isn't the best.[1]

When Criticism Isn't Constructive

When you read through some of the major newspapers, you'll notice many have critics. I'm not talking about readers who send in critical comments. These are people employed by the newspaper to point out what the writers and editors are doing wrong.

One of my friends was an opera critic for the *Los Angeles Times*. It was his job to attend productions, then write an article critiquing the performance, pointing out the strengths and the weaknesses. When I read the column, I usually had to use a dictionary to decipher what he was saying. Newspapers also have movie and restaurant critics. Some have a proclivity toward pointing out weaknesses and defects, while others look for the best. Each emphasizes something different.

There are other critics in life, as well. For some, it's a mother or father continually pointing out flaws. With a mother or father like this, you feel as though you're in court—only the judge is also the jury, and you have no assistance in defending yourself. He or she picks apart whatever you do, and makes sure you know how you messed up. It probably started at an early age, and as you grew, it shaped your core belief about yourself. Your parent truly may have wanted to motivate you to do your best. But the process was destructive.

Parents like this have the ability to throw verbal hand grenades. All too often, what we hear as children takes up permanent residence as an ever-present personal critic. We end up incorporating this criticism into our thought life.

Even if your parents are no longer alive, what they've said to you is probably still very much alive in your mind.

The inner critic that we have within us usually isn't objective. It tends to be biased toward the negative. And it continues to grow. Sometimes it whispers. At other times, it may almost shout. And it's responsible for the self-talk distortions that drag us down.

Many have told me they'd like to find an "off" switch for their mind. One woman said, "My mind seems to be an inner battleground. My mind has this tendency to be locked into a heartless, fearful, judgmental mode toward me, rather than in a loving, accepting, scriptural mode. How do I switch it?"

"I don't like to be judged. I didn't like when my mother or father did it, or my teachers and friends. But I especially don't like it when I do it to myself. Call it what you like—a critic or a judge. I feel like a prisoner in my own mind, and I'd like to be liberated."

Perhaps you can identify with this scenario:

You wake up earlier than you needed to and you lie there thinking, going over what you have facing you that day and what could go wrong. You feel anxiety about getting up and facing the day. You have good intentions about what to eat for breakfast, but when you use three spoons of sugar on your cereal and three in your coffee, you begin to feel guilty. You hear a voice in your head chiding, "You can't control what you eat, can you?"

When you arrive at work, your supervisor compliments you on what you did the day before, and says she's glad you're a part of the team. You appreciate the compliment, but your stomach churns as you fret, "What if I make a mistake today? What if . . . ?" and that critical voice inside you says once again, "You'll mess it up somehow."

A friend leaves a message on your phone saying she got the position she wanted . . . the one you'd hoped to land. You're upset that she got the job, and begin rehearsing verbal jabs you'd like to say, but know you won't. Your thoughts turn to why you'd never have gotten that position anyway. You look at your desk and think, "I'll never get all this done today. I should have stayed later last night, and gotten started on this . . ."

Uneasily, you wonder if you should call that potential new love interest. But you don't want to seem too eager, and you wonder if there's really any interest in you.

Snapping back to the present, you inwardly lament, "I'm wasting time again! What's wrong with me? I'll never get this work done! I'm really inefficient. I'll probably lose this job!" It's a message you heard years ago, over and over: Don't plan on landing a good job. You'll just lose it.

Now, *you* are the one telling it to yourself.

In *Soul Without Shame*, author Byron Brown suggests that you have a judge in your mind, presiding over a courtroom of life. Living through your body and your energy, this judge is "a master of words, and yet you can feel it in your belly, your shoulders, and your jaw." Brown says, "Sometimes, you feel accused of doing something wrong or unthinkable; at other times, you feel you have been caught red-handed. Sometimes, you present a case for your own guilt and corruption; at other times, you argue hard to justify your innocence."[2]

Whose voice do you hear with each self-judging statement within your own mind? Your own?

It is now. But who said it first? It could have been a parent, a teacher, or a sibling. After hearing it enough, you began to believe it as truth. But it isn't. Your worth is *not* based on these statements.

You've heard the word *corrosion*. It's not a very positive word. We usually think of it in terms of a crumbling pipe, or a deteriorating battery cable. The word actually means to eat away, weaken, or destroy gradually.

Unfortunately, there are many who are raised in a corrosive environment. The family may have been intact and finances stable, but the messages sent to the children were critical and toxic and eventually began to erode what each child believed, and how he or she felt about him- or herself. These messages gained a foothold and continued doing corrosive work for years.

A *depressogenic environment* occurs when a person isn't given adequate support for his self-esteem because of corrosive messages. This type of environment is contrary to the teaching of Scripture, which states that all believers are members of the body of Christ, and we're to encourage and build up one another.

In Colossians 3:21, parents are warned: "Fathers . . . [do not be hard on them (children) or harass them], lest they become discouraged and sullen and morose and feel inferior and frustrated. [Do not break their spirit.]" (AMP). Perhaps this was your experience.

As a child, you soak up verbal and nonverbal messages like a sponge. You listen to, watch, and imitate your parents. What you learn is engraved upon your mind.

The Negative Word We All *Should* Shed

Consider Laura's case. She was in her thirties and struggled with guilt constantly. She felt guilty over eating too much, spending too much, noticing good-looking men, leaving her children while she worked, and not "being spiritual" enough.

All of this came out in her automatic thoughts in the form of "should":

> I should be a better mother and not leave my children with a babysitter.
> I should go on a diet and lose fifteen pounds.
> I should get rid of my credit cards.
> I should think more about my husband's needs.
> I should read my Bible more.

What were all these "should" thoughts connected to? Some deep fears such as:

> If I don't spend more time with my children, they'll be messed up.
> If I don't lose weight, my husband may leave me.

(If "shoulds" are a part of your life, see the Statements Record at the end of this chapter.)

All of Laura's fears seemed unrealistic, but there was a reason for them. She believed she needed to be perfect in order to be accepted and loved. Where did this belief come from? Years of hearing her parents say, "You're fat," "You don't try hard enough," "You're not responsible."

Laura tried and tried to get their approval, but they never seemed pleased. So her list of "shoulds" grew and grew, as did her striving to be perfect. In her mind, being perfect led to being loved.

She also believed that God had rejected her because she wasn't a perfect Christian. She eventually gave up on God—in her mind, she could never measure up.

Many of us see God through our core beliefs, selecting certain passages of Scripture to justify those beliefs. But when we do that, what we believe is often not what Scripture teaches. This is why God's unconditional love is needed as the foundation for our core beliefs.

How Trauma Affects Core Beliefs

Traumatic events also affect core beliefs. A traumatic experience is something beyond our capability of handling. By definition, if you can "handle it," it's not a trauma.

But what does this have to do with our thought life? Well, trauma literally rewires the brain. It could be a death, an accident, physical or sexual abuse, neglect, or something else. If trauma occurs during early childhood, there are several results, including overdeveloping some of the neural networks related to survival, and actually retarding some aspects of growth, such as emotional development.

One of the other ways the brain responds to trauma is through imprinting. The more extensive the trauma, and the more frequently it occurs, the more of an imprint or indelible impression is left within the brain. Someone described trauma as actually tattooing the experience on the brain.

The imprint is a processing template through which new information to the brain is passed. Its effects are like this:

Imagine the brain as a large valley with a river running through it. Several streams converge into the river. Those are like the pathways in the brain. When a rainstorm—normal negative event—rips through the valley, the excess water flows in a predictable direction. It finds its way to creeks, then streams, and then converges into the river. But sometimes there is a massive storm that has so much rain, the runoff goes beyond existing channels and creates a new path outside the streams. It may even alter the course of the river in some way. Once the river has been changed, it tends to stay that way, until a more intense storm establishes a new channel.

In a similar way, everyday normal experiences come into the brain and find their way to existing networks or processing templates. All that changes if an overwhelming storm occurs. After that, alterations occur in thinking.

Childhood trauma is the equivalent of the 100-year flood.[3] New pathways are formed. The experience of trauma makes new imprints on the brain. And that can change thinking forever, unless steps are taken, usually through therapy, to reverse the damage.

When a child is traumatized, his brain literally forms itself around the experience it encounters. The experience is coded into neural templates. Any new experience similar to the original event will then create that same traumatic response.

How does this relate to our core beliefs and subsequent thoughts? Just imagine that you're a small child, and at an early age you begin to hear negative messages: "You're no good," "You're so awkward," "You can't be trusted," "You'll never amount to much."

You hear these negative messages over and over again, week after week, month after month, year after year. You hear them at a time when you and your brain are developing. Perhaps if you hear them only occasionally, there's not as much impact. But constant rejections eventually have an effect like the 100-year flood of trauma. When you hear the message again and again, it's as though a groove is gradually worn into the memory banks of your brain, and you begin to believe this is reality. You believe this is the truth. It becomes a core belief, shaping your thoughts and self-talk about who you really are.

Challenging Negative Core Beliefs

As you learn to change your self-talk and challenge your thoughts, it's important to discover where your core beliefs, the beliefs about yourself, originated. Often, they're negative:

I'm no good.
I'm inadequate.
I'm unlovable.
I'm worthless.
Others will always take advantage of me.
God will punish me.

These core beliefs, even though many are unhealthy, helped you make sense of your world when you were a child. And so they're carried with you through adolescence and into adulthood. We often think of them as absolute truths, though they were built in childhood. Left unchallenged, they continue to influence us throughout life.

Identifying core beliefs is a process. It helps to begin like this:

Each morning and evening, ask yourself: *What do I believe about myself?* Write whatever comes to mind. Then complete the statement, *This belief came from ...* Do this for a week.

What I believe about myself:

_____

_____

_____

_____

_____

_____

_____

_____

_____

_____

_____

This belief came from:

_____

_____

_____

For another week, ask yourself each morning and evening: *What do I believe about other people?* Again, write whatever comes to mind. Then complete the statement, *This belief came from . . .*

What I believe about other people:

_____

_____

_____

_____

_____

_____

_____

_____

_____

_____

This belief came from:

_____

_____

_____

For yet another week, ask yourself each morning and evening: *What do I believe about God?* Write what comes to mind. Then complete the statement, *This belief came from . . .*

What I believe about God:

_____

_____

_____

_____

_____

_____

_____

_____

This belief came from:

_____

_____

By exploring your core beliefs in this way, you'll be better prepared to respond to your inner critic. You can ask: Which core belief is prompting or creating this thought?

After identifying your core beliefs, the next step is to evaluate each one. Is it really true, or a distortion of the truth? You've been believing them for years, and you won't change them overnight. But change is possible. What it takes is evidence.

Evidence will show the belief isn't true, isn't accurate, and actually may be the opposite of what is true—there is actually evidence to the contrary.

As you notice negative self-talk stemming from a core belief, ask yourself, Where is the evidence that this belief is true? Also ask yourself, Where is the evidence this is false?

Your task is to keep track of *all* evidence that might disagree with your core beliefs, no matter how small or insignificant it seems to you. Just accumulate the evidence, and begin looking for truths that show the opposite could be true. Write it down, so you can refer to it later, as you begin to challenge these thoughts systematically and replace them with healthier, positive thinking.

Jenny came for her counseling appointment and was quite excited over her progress challenging her negative core beliefs:

"I experienced several negative 'put down' thoughts about myself because of some interactions at work," she reported. "Not only was I able to identify a core belief which created these thoughts, I even argued with that core belief and said it was wrong. That was a first for me! I've tried to confront those negative thoughts before, but now I'm able to deal with the underlying cause that's the culprit. I feel I'm on the right track. I feel hopeful."

When a crime has been committed, the police tenaciously gather minute pieces of evidence, in order to prove a case against the perpetrator. Their goals are not only to identify and apprehend the culprit, but also to build an ironclad case against him, using irrefutable evidence. Just think of yourself as a member of a crime-scene investigation team. You, too, are working toward discovery, conviction, and, in your case, freedom from your old thinking pattern.

A friend told me she began asking herself the question, Suppose I didn't believe the toxic belief that I'm a failure and always will be. Suppose the opposite *is* true. What would my thoughts and self-talk be like? How would I feel?

Then she formulated an opposite thought that was realistic and affirming. She was amazed when her feelings began to change as well. This can happen for you too.

It may help to formulate a core belief you'd like to have, then begin building the evidence for it. For instance, you may have been told for years that you're not capable of accomplishing great things. Your goal would be to debunk that, replacing it with the new core belief: I'm a capable, talented person!

Start by listing evidence showing your old core belief was wrong. Perhaps you've graduated from college with a 4.0 grade point average. Perhaps you placed second in a state piano competition. Perhaps you were selected for your job from a field of thirty applicants.

Next, build a case for the new belief. Write down even the smallest piece of evidence. Then, to really cement the change, read the list out loud. Remember, you need to hear the words to reinforce the truth and have it impact your brain in a more forceful way. This helps you really *believe* the evidence.

Practice Makes Perfect

Our emotions are initiated and escalated by what we say to ourselves about our parents, our spouse, our experiences, the past, the future, even God. The more emotion attached to an event, the more we tend to remember about it. The memory section of our brain comes into play here. Repeated self-talk, over time, turns into attitudes, values, and beliefs. Most of that comes from memories. And some self-talk comes by way of pictures flashing on our mind.

> Repeated self-talk, over time, turns into attitudes, values, and beliefs.

You may be thinking, Norm, you've already said this. You're just repeating yourself.

That's correct. And I'll keep doing that. I'm practicing an important principle in learning and change. It's called repetition. Without repetition and practice, there won't be any changes.

Do any of these statements sound familiar?

"You can't do anything right."

"You'll never be attractive—you won't find a mate."

"You never were much good."

"You're fortunate you got any kind of job."

"You'll always be a failure."

"Don't plan on college. You'll never get in."

These voices are your enemies. They're deceitful. They distort reality. They're nothing but lies. And they may be coming from *you*!

Unfortunately, if you said these once, you probably said or thought them hundreds of times. You used repetition to make these a part of your memory banks.

Now you can learn to use repetition in a positive way.

Go back to those messages. If any of those sound familiar, analyze them. Ask yourself about each:

1. Where is the evidence? What could show this belief is true? If I asked three of my friends, would they agree that this negative statement about me is true?
2. Is there evidence to the contrary? List things that show that the core belief is false.
3. If the belief really is true, what do you want to do to correct it?

Perhaps your core belief is that you can't do anything right. Try spending tomorrow telling yourself you can't do anything *wrong*. It may feel ridiculous to tell yourself that. But is it really any more ridiculous than the assumption that you can't do anything right?

If your self-talk often hammers you with "I can't do anything right," consider repeating to yourself instead: Sometimes I don't do things well. But most of the time, what I do is quite good.

You may tend to tell yourself: You'll never be attractive—you'll never find a mate. Instead, tell yourself: Some days I look good, and some days so-so—sort of like everyone else—and there *are* people interested in me.

The negative "You never were much good" could be flip-flopped to "I'm not perfect, but I have a number of positive qualities. God knows me, loves me, has sacrificed for me, and I am worth his attention. In his sight, I am really somebody."

"You're fortunate you got any kind of job" could be changed to "I'm grateful for having a job, and I am qualified for a number of jobs."

"You're a failure" could be changed to "Mistakes are learning experiences. They create valuable lessons. I may fail at some things, but that doesn't mean I'm a failure as a person."

Get the idea? Talk back to the old messages, those old lies.

You may be thinking, It won't work. Well, I've seen it work. Your negative self-talk may be screaming, I can't do it! Yes, you can. You can learn, practice, and change.

What God Says

Your thought life is not your own. It, like the rest of you, belongs to God.

If your thought life, your self-talk, is moving in the wrong direction, there's good news straight from God's Word. Scripture teaches that our thoughts *can* change.

In Philippians 4:8, we're told what the contents of our thoughts should be: "Finally, brothers, whatever is true, whatever is noble, whatever is right, whatever is pure, whatever is lovely, whatever is admirable—if anything is excellent or praiseworthy—think about such things" (NIV). And then Paul goes on to say the word I've been emphasizing, *practice*: "Whatever you have learned or received or heard from me, or seen in me—put it into practice. And the God of peace will be with you" (4:9).

In Ephesians 4:23, Paul talks about being renewed in the spirit of your minds. When you pray, ask God to renew your mind. Keep track of toxic messages from the past, challenge that damaging self-talk, and ask God to purge your memory banks of those false core beliefs. Your goal is to realize that God, through the power of his Holy Spirit, gives each person the ability to picture things in the way he pictures them. Every person needs a transformation of the mind in order to have the mind of Christ. The power of these passages is made possible through a personal relationship with Jesus Christ. This is how the reality of peace in our lives is finally realized.

Dr. Lloyd Ogilvie, the former chaplain of the US Senate, said, "Each of us needs to surrender our mind to God." Doing so is an opportunity for you to change messages that are keeping you stuck.

Can your messages change? Yes. Can your life change? Yes.[4]

You'll probably question and argue with statements about your old beliefs being false, and the new ones being true. Expect this. You're involved in changing some deep-seated beliefs about yourself, and probably other people, as well as about God. Remember that you're not alone in this process— all your beliefs can be run through the grid of Scripture to see what God says about you. Every core belief you have about yourself that is negative is probably contrary to Scripture's promises about the way God sees you.[5]

Reflect and Remember

1. What are the words you remember hearing again and
   again as a child?

   _____

   _____

2. When you hear a voice in your mind, whose voice is
   it?

   _____

3. Which of the statements you heard repeatedly as a child
   became core beliefs?

   _____

   _____

   _____

4. What are some core beliefs you'd like to change at this time?

   _____

   _____

   _____

5. What pictures reflect on your mind more than you would like?

   _____

   _____

6. Describe how you will make use of Philippians 4:8–9 and Ephesians 4:23.

   _____

   _____

7. Which of Laura's statements did you identify with?

   _____

   _____

8. What are three additional core beliefs you have about yourself?

   _____

   _____

   _____

9. Describe a friendly voice in your mind—one that offers friendly thoughts rather than toxic thoughts.

_____

_____

_____

Statements Record

During the coming week, record your "should" statements. In each case, record an alternative way of thinking about the same experience without using a "should."

Should Statement	Alternative

Self-Talk—Taking More Control

Fran was an attractive woman in her mid-thirties who longed to be in a serious, committed relationship headed toward marriage. Great guys asked her out. She liked them, and they liked her. But one after another, they fell like tin soldiers. And Fran had no idea that she was the one knocking them down—all because of her self-talk.

The pattern was always the same. As the relationship progressed, Fran began to retreat, even though the man in her life was involved and interested. Each in the series of suitors was left wondering what he'd done wrong. The truth was, he hadn't done anything that sabotaged the relationship. What went wrong was all in Fran's mind.

It's quite normal that Fran listened to carried-on conversations in her mind between herself and her love interest. But she'd take the smallest incident and let her mind wander with it. For example, if her boyfriend didn't spend a long time on the phone with her, she'd tell herself, He's losing interest!

Soon she'd be imagining all kinds of related problems in the relationship. Sometimes she ended up believing imagined offenses actually occurred. But that's the power of our self-talk.

While Fran can't see the destructiveness of her self-talk, Tom recognizes the harmful potential of his self-talk. In frustration, he calls it "chatter."

"That's the best word I can use to describe what goes on in my head," he says. "It's my own, I realize, but sometimes it involves others. I actually carry on full-length conversations in my head with others. Sometimes they're repetitive.

"I wish I could say they're good conversations, but most of the time they're not. Sometimes I chatter when I'm trying to go to sleep, and then I'm wide awake for hours. My body and my emotions are activated by that dumb, imagined conversation.

"There are times when I get angry or depressed and wonder why, but then it dawns on me—it's what I was thinking about! Does everyone do this, or am I the only one? I guess it's something we don't talk about."

I've said it before, but it's worth repeating: It's normal to talk to yourself. And you *can* learn to control your self-talk. In fact, by now, I hope you're already making progress. But to move farther along the journey, it will help to understand it even better.

"Chewing" on Our Thoughts

All day long we carry on conversations with ourselves. You may even find yourself talking out loud, or mumbling to yourself while you're having a dialogue with yourself.

We talk to ourselves while taking a shower or shaving or driving or listening to a lecture or a sermon. And sometimes we engage in self-talk without realizing we're doing it. We catch ourselves, and "vow" not to waste any more time doing it. But we will . . . and it's not always a waste of time.

Were you aware that talking to yourself is a habit you've cultivated? Think of your mind as a massive iPod, and over the year you've downloaded hundreds of statements that you can play at will. Some of them you've played so much that you're not really needed to tap the play button anymore. Now, you hear them automatically.

The more these play, the more we begin to believe them. We think, This is reality! This is true!

When we dwell continuously on the same theme or issue, it can be described as ruminating. This word came from a Latin word for "chewing the cud." If you've been around cows, you'll have a visual picture of what this means. It seems like some cows can go all day long chewing and chewing.

When we ruminate on a thought, we go over it again and again, often too many times to count. Ruminating reinforces that thought, the belief, and the effect. It can get in the way of reality. It also can get in the way of finding a solution to the problem.

Ruminating on a negative thought can cripple our creative thinking and hinder us from making positive steps. And several

> Another study showed that those who ruminate about their problems are four times more likely to develop major depression than those who don't.

studies have identified the link between rumination and depression. In 1989, there was a major earthquake in San Francisco. Those who ruminated about the experience were more likely to experience depression and post-traumatic stress. Another study showed that those who ruminate about their problems are four times more likely to develop major depression than those who don't.[1]

Even when you're not aware of the content of your self-talk, and even when some is negative, it's not a cause for concern. But help is needed when your negative thoughts become frequent, or when you believe negative thoughts that aren't really true, or when what you tell yourself goes against Scripture.

In an earlier chapter, we called these "toxic thoughts." They're not based in reality. They're distorted.[2] And by changing them, you can change your life.

The Power of Self-Talk

Is our self-talk all that important? Absolutely. What you say to yourself can control and direct your life, build or destroy relationships, determine whether you'll fail or succeed. The way you express anger, your ways of showing love, and how you handle conflict all are driven by self-talk.

Your self-talk may be based upon some of your attitudes. A positive attitude toward self tends to generate positive self-talk, while a negative attitude generates negative self-talk.

Self-talk is *based* on your beliefs. And what you truly believe is manifested in both your inner and oral conversations.

Listen to these thoughts:

Jim, a high school teacher: There's no point in figuring out what I want since I don't deserve it anyway. And even if I deserve it, I won't get it.

Joan, a mother of three: I am going through life with a chip on my shoulder. I'm always angry.

Don, a salesperson: Anything I tackle has got to fail.

Gina, a financial analyst: I run everything through a negative filter.

Ann, a stay-at-home mom: I always feel guilty, no matter what I do.

Sam, a contractor: Nothing ventured, nothing lost. That's my motto. I'm afraid to try for failing.

Trent, a music student: What I don't like is me.

Mary, a waitress: What's wrong with me! I'm never content. When am I going to be happy?[3]

Do any of these sound familiar? Have you made similar statements? By repeating this kind of self-talk, we allow it to shape our lives.

In my experiences as a counselor, I've found that most people seem to believe that outside events, other people, and circumstances determine their emotions, behaviors, and verbal responses. Those things certainly do influence us. But it's our thoughts that are usually the source of how we feel, behave, and speak.

Even if our thoughts are irrational, we tend to believe them. What we think about things and people will determine the emotions we feel, and the behaviors and verbal responses we express.

We prefer to think others are the problem. It's easier to blame than to say, "It's me." Instead we say, "I'm right and you're wrong. I'm not the one who needs to change."

As an example of how your beliefs affect your self-talk, consider these typical beliefs about marriage (we'll talk more about marriage later):

My spouse should make me happy.

My spouse should meet all my needs.

My spouse should know what my needs are without my having to tell him/her.

My spouse should be willing to do things according to my way of doing them.

My spouse should not respond in an irritable or angry way to me.

Do these statements build a marriage or create problems? Do these statements reflect self or grace?

If you have any of these beliefs, you'll find that each will lead to one thought after another. Those thoughts become increasingly intense, inflammatory, and stress-producing. You may even carry on imaginary conversations between yourself and your spouse and later believe the conversations actually took place.

Now let's assume these beliefs were true in your marriage. What do you think you would be saying to yourself? Write out your response for each one.

1. _____

2. _____

3. _____

4. _____

5. _____

Let's consider for a moment this exchange between a husband and wife and discover the self-talk that prompted it:

It's Saturday morning, 11 a.m., and Frank strolls into the kitchen yawning and half dressed.

> Pam: It's about time you got up. It looks like you're going to waste the entire day!
>
> Frank (looking a bit startled): What's with you? I'm just taking my time getting up and enjoying a day off.
>
> Pam: That's just it. You're around here so rarely, and half the day is shot! By the time you get dressed and cleaned up, lunch will be over and nothing has been accomplished!
>
> Frank: Who said I was getting dressed and cleaned up? The only thing I want to accomplish is a cup of coffee, the paper, and the football game on TV!

Pam: What? I don't get a day off! We have a whole list of work to be done here. When *are* you going to do it?

Frank: I suppose you've been saving up a list of work projects again. Why don't you give me some notice ahead of time? If I wanted to work today, I could go into the shop and get overtime, plus some peace and quiet!

What's happening in this conversation? First of all, each person has an unspoken expectation for Saturday. One for work, one for pleasure. Problems like this can be eliminated if individuals clarify their expectations in advance.

Let's look at Pam's self-talk. She was expecting her husband to accomplish a number of tasks on Saturday. She got up at 6:30 and began having this inner conversation:

7:30 I hope he gets up pretty soon. I'd like to get started on these projects. With the kids away today, we can get a lot done.

8:15 Ya know, I don't hear a sound. Well, I'm going to start work in the yard. He'll probably hear me and then he can join me.

9:15 What time is it? 9:15! I don't believe it! He's sleeping away the morning. Who does he think he is? How thoughtless! I ought to go in there and wake him up!

10:00 Just because he has no work at the plant or at church, he thinks he's entitled to sack out. What about me? When do I ever get to do this? He ticks me off! He probably knows I want him to take care of those chores he's been putting off. He just wants to ignore them as well as me!

10:45 How could he be so insensitive? Look at all I do for him!

What type of emotions do these statements arouse? What kind of behaviors do you think these statements prompt? What kind of communication is happening?

Suppose instead she chose thoughts such as the following:

7:30 I wish he'd get up. I think I'll check and see if he's just resting or sleeping.

8:15 I'm not sure he's going to get up in time to do much today. I'd better revise my list, and then ask him if he could help me with these two chores after lunch.

9:15 I'm a bit upset with him, but I have to admit, I didn't tell him I wanted him to work today. Next time, I'll talk it over with him before the weekend.

10:00 I could serve him breakfast in bed when he wakes up. When's the last time I did that?

Two very different styles of self-talk. The choice is ours whether to make our self-talk positive or negative.

Here are some other typical thoughts that will probably enter your mind at one time or another:

My spouse will never change. He/she will always be that kind of person.

I can never meet my spouse's needs.

If I bring up that subject, my spouse will just get mad again.

Why bother asking him/her to share his/her feelings? He/she will only clam up again.

He hates me.

I just know there's an affair going on.

He's so inconsiderate! Why doesn't he grow up?

I must have everything perfect in my house.

These are thoughts I've heard from many over the years. What do you think each statement would do to your emotional state? To your relationship with the other person?

Self-talk generates and creates mental pictures in our mind. As mental pictures begin to emerge, the imagination is called into action. We've talked about this before. As we run mental pictures through the panoramic screen of our mind, our self-talk is expanded and reinforced.

> The choice is ours whether to make our self-talk positive or negative.

Listen . . . to Yourself!

Listening is the foundation of communication. Without good listening, relationships fail.

We've all heard admonishments to listen to one another, to be "good listeners." I'm going to encourage you to do the same, but not with regard to others. I'd like you to listen to *yourself*.

It's important to hear what you're saying to yourself. Listen for negative thoughts, misbeliefs, or toxic, distorted statements. Pay attention to your self-talk. What is it about? Who is it directed toward? God? Your spouse? Children?

When you're having a difficult time interacting with another person, what are you saying to yourself at that time? Since many of these thoughts are automatic, they're occurring internally while you carry on the other conversation with another person. It's important to listen to your self-talk—it will help you to be aware of the content, and know whether it's mostly positive or negative.

Develop a new habit called Self-Talk Awareness (STA). Make an agreement with yourself to become more aware of your inner dialogue.

Develop a reminder system. Place notes to yourself in appropriate places such as the car, bathroom, fridge, purse, briefcase. Any constant visual reminders will work. On small cards, jot down one or two words, each summarizing your self-talk, such as "Distorted," or "Not true."

Keep this with you at all times in your pocket, purse, or briefcase. Seeing this in print will have a greater impact. This is just to make you more aware of how busy your mind is. Evaluate what you've written down. Is it realistic, the truth, positive, constructive? Or is it negative, a misbelief, or toxic?

If it's not what you want or like, don't get down on yourself. This is not a time of evaluation, but of awareness. Don't become critical of yourself. It's likely that you're too critical of yourself already.

It's also important to listen to your body. Have you ever experienced your body becoming tense, your shoulders sore, your stomach churning or turning over, your fists clenched, or finding yourself holding your breath? Thoughts create physical responses as well. Your self-talk can create tension in your body, increase blood pressure and heart rate, upset your stomach, and trigger a variety of emotional responses.[4]

When Self-Talk Leads You Astray

Let's consider another facet of self-talk. It drifts. And as a drifting boat can get into trouble, so can the mind.

Thoughts also wander. Sometimes there's more energy involved in wandering. It can be more active than drifting. We say of a child, "he wandered away," or remark that a husband "wandered from the marriage."

We all have wandering minds. Even when you're focused on a particular subject or speaker or engaged in a personal activity, your mind may wander away from your intended purpose. It's easy to begin daydreaming, planning, fantasizing, or just aimlessly drifting about.

The other day, I asked a friend if his mind ever wandered. He looked at me as if I should know it does! He barked, "Wander! Does it wander! It's wandering around somewhere in the desert, and I haven't seen it for years!"

Wandering and getting absorbed in other things is what our minds do. But sometimes our minds wander into areas that feed our problems, rather than help resolve them. For example, if you're having problems in your marriage, allowing yourself to think about an attractive person at work isn't a helpful use of your thoughts.

Sometimes we can become entangled where we've allowed ourselves to drift: to future events, past painful encounters, worries, and so on.

God understands. Consider this Scripture:

And you, Solomon my son, know the God of your father [have personal knowledge of Him, be acquainted with, and understand Him; appreciate, heed, and cherish Him] and serve Him with a blameless heart and a willing mind. For the Lord searches all hearts and minds and understands all the *wanderings* of the thoughts. If you seek Him [inquiring for and of Him, and requiring Him as your first and vital necessity] you will find Him; but if you forsake Him, He will cast you off forever! (1 Chron. 28:9 AMP, emphasis added)

I might not be aware of all my thoughts, but God certainly is. He "understands all the wanderings of the thoughts."

When I'm listening to the Sunday sermon, or to someone who's telling a novel-length story, my mind wanders. Does yours? Where does it go? Probably to something that's pleasant or of more interest.

Do *you* ever find your mind wandering when you're trying to meditate or pray? Of course you do. We engage in meditation or prayer with the best of intentions. Our mind is so busy and active we look forward to a time of peace and quiet, a respite from too much brain activity. And we focus . . . for a minute or so. And then our mind takes off in another direction altogether.

As you become more aware of how your mind sabotages your good intentions to meditate on God's Word or spend ten minutes in concentrated prayer, you make a discovery. Your mind has "a mind of its own," so to speak. Regardless of your good intentions to keep it under control and in balance, it still wanders away into thoughts about the past, future, pain, or loss.

This tendency is normal. It doesn't need to be "fixed."

I think it's safe to say that most of us struggle with our prayer life in this way. We begin with a clear focus. But somewhere along the way, we get off the main highway and onto a side road, and we wander until we realize what we've done. We quickly return to our praying. But in time, we end up thinking about a task or an involvement with another person or what needs to be done. The vicious cycle begins. We start to berate ourselves for our lack of discipline and spirituality. Then guilt creeps in. What started out as a conversation with God turns into a bout with negative self-talk.

If this sounds familiar, there is a way to enrich your prayer life and make it meaningful. First, make a list of prayer concerns, and use it each time you pray. If possible, obtain pictures of people for whom you're praying, and look at the pictures as you pray. Pray aloud, rather than to yourself. Hearing your voice keeps you more centered. By using your eyes, as well as your ears, you're more focused and attentive in your praying.

It's not necessary to stop the wandering. Instead, accept its presence, and discover where it takes you. It doesn't help to become angry and frustrated over it.

You can learn to notice your wandering. As soon as you realize your mind is drifting, just accept it. You don't want to create a battleground for your mind. Fighting your wandering mind may make it wander even more.

It's difficult to slow yourself down to meditate, pray, or even concentrate on reading something (such as this book!). Everyone's mind wanders. So relax. You're normal.

But you can learn to realize more quickly that your mind is wandering. Once that happens, decide whether you want to let it wander, or bring it back to the subject at hand.

When you catch your mind wandering, identify where it went. What *were* you thinking about? You might even choose to let your mind and thoughts wander for a specific purpose. I do, especially when I'm in the midst of writing a book—it becomes a positive, creative experience.

On other occasions, wandering wastes your time. Even worse, at times, wandering is negative, detrimental, and counterproductive. For example, if you have only an hour to complete a project, and your mind wanders for thirty minutes, will the result be good? Probably not.

Simply becoming aware of wandering is the first step to having greater control. You might decide to allow about thirty to sixty seconds of mind-wandering. Then you can bring yourself back to focusing on the task at hand, telling yourself, Now that I've got that out of my system, I can concentrate.[5]

Memories, and How They Affect Self-Talk

Memories affect our self-talk profoundly. Life is made up of memories. Without them life is incomplete.

Over time, memories fade. They lose their sharpness. They may need photos or someone's reminder to activate them. But sometimes sights, sounds, and smells of an event can affect us more than we want, bringing long-forgotten memories sharply into focus.

Anyone who has experienced a trauma—a serious accident, violence, witnessing the World Trade Center towers crumbling in New York—has memories that, when activated, create panic or bring back the feelings from when the event actually occurred.

Self-talk comes from memories.

For example, you have memories of your parents, and they reflect who you are today. Those memories hold emotions you had as a child. They also contain the statements you heard.

Memories are made up of bits and pieces from what we remember of the past. They're not based entirely on facts. They're more like a collage, including feelings, images, perspectives, and fragments, all spread out on a table and pieced together to make what becomes our life story. It's our history, and it helps us make sense of our lives.

It doesn't matter who your parents were. It matters who you *remember* they were. What would you have said about your parents twenty years ago? Ten years ago? Five years ago? What would you have said about your life twenty years ago? Ten years ago? Five years ago? You probably had different versions. There might be different themes and issues. Changes occur. Those memories are the basis for some of your self-talk.

The fading of memories can bring about healing. In her book *I Thought We'd Never Speak Again*, Laura Davis writes, "Old hurts, which seemed huge and insurmountable at one time, often recede to the back burner after a number of years as we gather new experiences in life; we frequently view the old ones from a different perspective when we are open to the changing landscape. Our lives can expand in ways that previously seemed impossible."[6]

But the phrase "Time heals all wounds" isn't always true. Time isn't always a healer. Memories of hurts can feed the self-talk running through our minds. Your pain can even grow, if those thoughts are fed and intensified.

On the other hand, when you add new, accurate self-talk to the passing of time, the intensity of the feelings can be blunted. It helps to say something like: *That happened in the past. This is what's happening today.*

It's up to you. Will you mellow over time and move on? Or will you hold on to hurts, becoming bitter and stuck? Some people are so determined to hold on to childhood pain, they allow their parents to control their life and relationships even when they're seventy!

Over the years, I've worked with many individuals who've experienced crisis or trauma. When this occurs, we move into a survival mode. We put into place a psychological defense system. We choose either the "fight" (stay and deal with it) or "flight" (run like crazy) response.

What triggers this defense system? It's usually activated by fearful or anxious thoughts. When this happens, it causes the production of stress chemicals that gets us ready for moving into action. And that can cause an imbalance of chemicals in our brains.

But the response isn't triggered by the crisis. It's triggered by what we *think* about the crisis.

Our thoughts create these emotions, not reality. You may not even be in a bad situation, but if you think you are, you respond as if you were. Once again we see the power of our thoughts.[7]

Sometimes we react to a real event, and sometimes to an imagined one. Why can't our mind tell the difference between the two? It seems the brain should be able to look at its storehouse of memories and say, "This one is real," and "This one isn't real."

> You may not even be in a bad situation, but if you think you are, you respond as if you were.

But it's not an absolute retrieval system. Sometimes brain cells respond to something close to the real thing. This is why we're sometimes triggered into fight-or-flight mode, even when there's no real reason for it.[8]

How can we diffuse the power of well-established negative thinking patterns? What works for one individual may not work for another.

Your brain sits ready to do your bidding. When you think a thought (whether you want to or not), it ends up as a specific instruction to your brain. If you think a pleasant thought, your brain picks it up and runs with it to other similar thoughts stored in its vault. If you think an angry thought, or a depressive thought, it does the same.

When your new thought connects with others that are stored there, it intensifies because of your accumulated memories.

If you struggle with a number of these during the day, no wonder you're upset. What's the answer? Choose to think thoughts that don't contain memory banks. It could be just a simple, neutral thought, or even something nonsensical. There's no negative memory banks to activate.[9] And that diffuses the effect of the negative thoughts that have been intensifying.

By repeatedly expressing the new thought you choose— out loud—you zap the power of toxic thoughts.

You're not a victim of your self-talk. Change is possible. It's a slow process. But hopefully, you've started the process already. Let it continue.

Reflect and Remember

1. What comes to mind when you think of these key words from this chapter?
   chatter
   ruminating
   inner conversation
   wandering

   _____

   _____

2. Do you catch yourself "ruminating"? _____
   Place a picture of a cow in an obvious place to remind you not to "chew on" negative self-talk.

3. What are some of your beliefs that generate your self-talk?

   _____

   _____

4. What steps can you take to develop STA (Self-Talk Awareness)?

_____

_____

5. James 1:19 says, "Be a ready listener" (AMP). Listen to your own conversations with yourself.

6. If you think you're the only one who struggles with a wandering mind, ask friends, family, or people in your small group if it happens to them too. They may share surprising—and valuable—insight.

7. Which suggestions about wandering thoughts or prayer will you implement this week?

_____

_____

8. Describe memories that feed your self-talk.

_____

_____

_____

_____

6

Igniting Change—
What's Holding You Back?

Gail is part of a successful theater group. She's even won accolades for her roles. It's a dream come true for her—one that almost didn't happen.

A few years ago, she only dreamed of being an actress. It was something she'd wanted to try since childhood. But she'd always been held back by two powerful things—what she believed about herself, and what she told herself.

For years, she lamented her missed chance to do the one thing she really wanted to do. Finally, a friend confronted her. She bluntly told Gail, "You need to stop whining about not being able to act, and just do something about it!"

Gail began to evaluate her beliefs about herself and her critical voice. She finally decided that all those old reasons she'd always told herself—the self-talk about why she couldn't act—might not be true. She swallowed down her fear and tried out for a part in a small play . . . and she did well! Her acting opportunities grew rapidly after that first successful show.

Now when others ask about Gail's success, her answer is simply, "I changed my thoughts, and my life changed."

Most of us will admit to being a "work in progress." And sometimes, that "work" being accomplished, as we move toward positive change, isn't pretty.

It's like the shaping of a country. When you read books on the history of any nation on earth, you'll realize that struggle and conflict were an important part of the process of making that country what it is. The pictures may depict bloody battles or massive devastation. It was what was required for change to occur.

Many live their daily life with a constant war—their battleground is their mind. For some, the result is tension and stress. For others, trauma creates wounds that linger for years, or even decades.

For many, making peace with their mind is just an elusive fantasy. Even brief times of peace are rare. As in any war, there are advances and victories, retreats and defeats.

The Bible acknowledges our inner conflicts. The apostle Paul openly describes his personal struggles in Romans 7:15–19:

> For I do not understand my own actions [I am baffled, bewildered]. I do not practice or accomplish what I wish, but I do the very thing that I loathe [which my moral

instinct condemns]. Now if I do [habitually] what is contrary to my desire, [that means that] I acknowledge and agree that the Law is good (morally excellent) and that I take sides with it. However, it is no longer I who do the deed, but the sin [principle] which is at home in me and has possession of me. For I know that nothing good dwells within me, that is, in my flesh. I can will what is right, but I cannot perform it. [I have the intention and urge to do what is right, but no power to carry it out.] For I fail to practice the good deeds I desire to do, but the evil deeds that I do not desire to do are what I am [ever] doing. (AMP)

Many of us can relate. We think, I want to change for the better, but I don't do it. What's wrong with me?

Listen to the answer in God's Word:

For those who are according to the flesh and are controlled by its unholy desires set their minds on and pursue those things which gratify the flesh, but those who are according to the Spirit and are controlled by the desires of the Spirit set their minds on and seek those things which gratify the [Holy] Spirit. Now the mind of the flesh [which is sense and reason without the Holy Spirit] is death [death that comprises all the miseries arising from sin, both here and hereafter]. But the mind of the [Holy] Spirit is life and [soul] peace [both now and forever]. [That is] because the mind of the flesh [with its carnal thoughts and purposes] is hostile to God, for it does not submit itself to God's Law; indeed it cannot. (Rom. 8:5–7 AMP)

And so the battle of our mind rages on and on. Why? It's simple. We have a sinful nature. But that *can* be overcome.

But no one promised it would be easy to change the way you are. And men and women give many reasons as to why they can't change their self-talk.

Whenever you say, "I can't do this," your words go from your mouth, into your ears, and to your brain, where they stick. The more you say this to yourself, the more you believe it. Eventually, it can immobilize you.

When you say you can't, you can't. It's just that simple. But remember Gail? Imagine harnessing that same power of saying, Yes I can!

Choosing to Change Self-Talk

"I can't" is a comfortable excuse. But it's not truth.

You'd be truthful in saying, "I choose *not* to change."

Perhaps that uncomfortable reality will spur you to say this, instead of "I can't": "I choose to change with God's help!"

Sometimes we don't see how we're feeding our problems and keeping them alive. Perhaps you've thought in frustration,

> Sometimes we don't see how we're feeding our problems and keeping them alive.

I don't like my toxic thoughts! It doesn't make sense to have a mind filled with negative messages. I understand this has been with me a long time, but I'd like it out of my life. What am I doing to keep it alive?

For years, Gail listened to her own critical thoughts about herself. It paralyzed her and kept her from pursuing her heart's desire . . . until she decided to challenge those negative thoughts.

Sometimes we inadvertently feed our problems and keep them alive. Even when we say we want to change! For years, Gail had done that without realizing it. Fortunately, her friend confronted her, and she turned that thinking around.

Can you think of examples of how you might be sabotaging yourself in the following ways? Jot them down in the space provided:

- repeating negative messages to yourself when feeling stressed, anxious, hurt, etc.

- regretting the past or worrying about the future

- setting unrealistic expectations for yourself

- choosing behaviors that support these negative beliefs

- criticizing, negating, and discounting yourself

  _____

  _____

- avoiding risks

  _____

  _____

  _____

- discounting feelings

  _____

  _____

- having relationships and spending time with negative and critical people

  _____

  _____

- comparing yourself to others

  _____

  _____

- self-criticism

  _____

  _____

- making choices that don't correspond to your values and beliefs

----

If you've identified with any of these, choose to stop feeding negative messages about yourself. Write your concerns on a prayer list, and ask God to intervene, and to remind you to challenge your self-talk each time you begin to respond in this way. Read your prayers aloud. Commit to stop feeding your toxic thoughts.

Remember that in order for your thought life to change, the old pattern of thinking needs to be evicted. Bringing positive realistic thoughts into your mind, while the old pattern of thinking is still functioning, won't work. The new, positive thoughts quickly become contaminated.

Think about your thought life in this way: Your toxic or negative self-talk can be represented by a glass of sour milk. Your positive and realistic self-talk can be a glass of fresh milk.

If you pour the glass of fresh milk into the container with the sour milk, would you drink it? Doubtful. It would still taste sour. The fresh milk has been ruined.

Even if you put the glass of sour milk in the bottom of a glass the size of an empty swimming pool and filled it with fresh milk, you'd still be wary. Sure, the sour milk would be very diluted. But the sour milk would quickly pollute the fresh. No matter how big the glass, the fresh milk would still be ruined by the sour.

It's the same principle with our thoughts. As long as any negative self-talk remains, it infects the positive. The effectiveness of the positive thoughts is greatly diminished. The negative thoughts that have been there for years need to be discarded.[1] Completely.

The Problem of "Shoulds"

I need to mention again how "shoulds" affect toxic thinking.

The effect of "shoulds" in our self-talk creeps in subtly. We may not use the word itself. But substitute words or phrases can be just as negative. We may also ask questions of ourselves that carry the same negative message, disapproving of behavior by asking a question that implies the "should":

> How could I have done that?
>
> Why didn't I think of that ahead of time?
>
> How could I be so stupid?
>
> Why didn't I plan ahead?
>
> I should not be that way.
>
> I should not have done that.
>
> I should have thought of that.

Sometimes we're not aware of the "shoulds" we speak—we just use them out of habit.

Shoulds can limit our growth and control our lives. They feed guilt and self-condemnation. And so often, there's no truth to them.

Learning to Reframe Your Self-Talk

Ready to take another step in banishing your negative self-talk and its toxic effects? There's an easy way. It's called reframing. It means putting a different spin or twist on an existing idea to give it new meaning.

Reframing can be a powerful tool in changing your self-talk. Reframing your self-talk gives it a realistic balance and positive emphasis.

You may tell yourself frequently: I'm really struggling with understanding my job.

You can reframe in a positive way by making a point to tell yourself: I enjoy my job. I know what the problems are. In time, I can work through them.

> Reframing your self-talk gives it a realistic balance and positive emphasis.

You may tell yourself frequently: I always seem to have a hard time getting through to her!

This can be changed to: I do want to hear her side, and I am a good listener. This relationship has the potential to be a good one.

You might say often: Today was a rough day. I sure hope things get better!

This can be changed to: Today had its challenges, but I made it through, just like the other days. I can work at making tomorrow better.

If you often tell yourself: I have a hard time with money. I'd like to save some. I always just spend it.

You can reframe by telling yourself: I earn good money. I can learn to put some aside each week. In time, I'll have quite a bit in the bank.

If you tell yourself: I'm so sloppy. The house is always a mess!

This can be changed to: I'm learning to be neat. There are times when this place looks good, and I know I can improve.

Can You Change?

It's up to you. You have several choices facing you as you consider changing your self-talk. Let's consider the options:

You could start and become 4discouraged, and reinforce your negative self-talk about yourself.

You could say, Why try, if it's so ingrained?

Or you could see changing your self-talk as an opportunity to grow and change your life. You could discover the exceptions to what you say, and reinforce those.

If you choose to try, change *will* occur. That's a fact. Quickly? No. That too is a fact.

In his book *Come Before Winter*, Charles Swindoll wrote:

Change—real change—takes place slowly. In first gear, not overdrive. Far too many Christians get discouraged and give up. Like ice skating or mastering a musical instrument or learning to water ski, certain techniques have to be discovered and developed in the daily discipline of living. Breaking habit patterns you established during the passage of years cannot occur in a few brief days. Remember that. "Instant" change is as rare as it is phony.[2]

It's true. Change takes time, and it can be hard, painful, discouraging, and difficult. We as a culture don't like the word *slow*. We want instant results. When it comes to changing your self-talk, that won't happen.

Do you know what the word *change* means? It means to make different, to give a different course or direction, to replace one thing with another, to make a shift from one to another, to undergo transformation, transition, or substitution.

However, to most people change is negative, something that implies inferiority, inadequacy, and failure. No wonder so many people resist the idea of change. Who wants to feel inferior and inadequate? But think of the alternative. What's the cost of not changing?

Change is growth.

How do you respond to these words?

become	expand	develop	enlarge	swell
augment	supplement	extend	mature	advance
bud	shoot up	progress	thrive	bear fruit
prosper	flourish	luxuriate	bloom	blossom

Each of these words is a synonym for *grow*, a word that describes *positive change*. Most people's response to the word *grow* is much more positive than it is to the word *change*. Yet without change there is no growth.

In a radio broadcast, Bible teacher Warren Wiersbe said this about change:

> We can benefit from change. Anyone who has ever really lived knows that there is no life without growth. When

we stop growing, we stop living and start existing. But there is no growth without change, there is no challenge without change. Life is a series of changes that create challenges, and if we are going to make it, we have to grow.[3]

Joseph Shore said it this way: "People are a lot like trees; they either grow or die. There's no standing still. A tree dies when its roots become blocked. God has made us in such a way that we become mentally, spiritually and eventually, physically dead when we choose to allow the circumstances of our lives to keep us from growing. Pastors, physicians and psychologists spend their lives trying to help individuals and institutions that have chosen to stop growing."[4]

Practice, Practice, Practice

For change to occur, we must practice . . . and keep practicing. There's that word again. *Practice*.

It's the reason some individuals rise to the top of their profession, when others don't. It's not just a matter of basic, raw talent. Consider the findings of Geoff Colvin in the book *Talent Is Overrated*. In looking at outstanding sports figures, as well as musicians, he suggests, the difference that accounts for their success over that of their peers is *not* talent, but practice. Even for those with an abundance of natural, above-average talent, that wasn't enough. To rise above, they had to put forth ongoing, consistent practice. It was demanding. It wasn't easy. Research showed that what separated the average musician or sports star from the better, and then the best, was practice. Deliberate practice.[5]

You know what practice is. You've done it and so have I. I grew up "practicing piano." For ten years! Some days I applied myself for that hour, and I improved. Other days, I went through the motions, daydreaming and watching the clock. "Deliberate practice" is the type of practice that is *designed* to improve what it is that you're doing. In most ventures, "designed" means having another person work with you, such as a teacher or coach or mentor or counselor. They can see what you cannot see, and can suggest improvements to your practicing.

In his book, Colvin describes it this way:

> It's apparent why becoming significantly good at almost anything is extremely difficult without the help of a teacher or coach, at least in the early going. Without a clear, unbiased view of the subject's performance, choosing the best practice activity will be impossible; for reasons that may be simply physical (as in sports) or deeply psychological, very few of us can make a clear, honest assessment of our own performance. Even if we could, we could not design the best practice activity for that moment in our development—the type of practice that would put us on the road to achieving at the highest levels—unless we had extensive knowledge of the latest and best methods for developing people in our chosen field. Most of us don't have that knowledge.[6]

This even applies to changing our self-talk. Whether it's a trusted, insightful friend, a counselor, a spouse, a teacher, or a sponsor, working with someone who can assist you, so you're not working alone, is important.

Deliberate practice means identifying what needs to be improved. It also means there's an element of high repetition.

In changing your self-talk, it's not enough to identify healthy realistic thoughts and repeat them once. Because of how deeply entrenched our old, toxic thoughts are, we may need to say the new ones hundreds of times before we truly change our thinking for the better.

> Because of how deeply entrenched our old, toxic thoughts are, we may need to say the new ones hundreds of times before we truly change our thinking for the better.

But this is nothing compared to the thousands of times the old statements have been expressed. Before you give up, because this sounds excessive, remember this *is* possible. Others have done this with great success. It *will* work!

Deliberate practice involves constant feedback. You need to see that this effort makes a difference. As you practice reframing your self-talk in a positive light, take note of the changes in your emotions and behavior.

Make a list of possible helpers, who are both good listeners and encouragers. Explain to them what you need. Describe what you are doing, and ask for their honest feedback, as well as reinforcement of your changes.

Deliberate practice will stretch your brainpower. It's hard mental work. You'll be working against what your brain is used to doing, countering the direction your brain is used to going.

Old patterns of thinking need to be discarded on the spot. One way is to write down the thought you want to discard, then wad it up. Either throw it in the trash or burn it. It also will help to practice the writing exercises in this book, and to talk with your helper.

Don't expect practice to be enjoyable or fun. It's effort. It's work. And sometimes, you may question its effectiveness. But keep your long-term goal in sight.

Getting Your New Lines Just Right

Most of us not only have to practice in order to learn, we need to review again and again. We have to rehearse. As an actor learns his lines for a play or a film, he goes over them again and again. That allows them to go from being words on a page to becoming part of him. They take on a life of their own.

It's the same with the new phrases you're speaking to yourself. They need to become a part of your life. The first time you go over one in your mind, you may feel awkward. It doesn't feel like it's "really you" yet. But the more you practice your new responses, the more they become the new you.

Years ago, when I was a student at Westmont College, I heard a chapel speaker who said, "If you read the same chapter from Scripture out loud every day for a month, that chapter will be yours for life." He was right. A number of us took him up on his suggestion and found that it worked.

It's the same with your self-talk. Think of this—the repeating of positive thoughts about yourself, in place of the old negative ones—as a rehearsal for living your life in a new way.

You've landed a part in a play. It's your big chance. You've dreamed of an opportunity such as this for years. In two months, the play opens. So, what do you do in the meantime? Sit around and wait? Work more at your daytime job? Wait until the night before the play opens? Not at all!

Your work is just beginning. You need to rehearse! You'll spend hours reading your lines, talking them out, and putting inflection and emotion into them to make them come alive.

Once that happens, can you relax? Probably not, for you can always refine and improve.

Rehearsals are a part of life. Musical groups spend hours a day in rehearsal for a three-minute selection. Sports teams spend weeks in training camps, getting ready for the season, going over their plays again and again. It's the only way for the athletes to improve and get in shape.

We rehearse presentations for work, for job interviews, for classes, for preaching sermons, for more things than we even realize.

We rehearse conversations in our minds—conversations with those who have offended us, angered us, frustrated us, or ignored us. We go over what happened (with embellishments, of course), and rehearse what we would like to say in future interactions, carefully choosing words that will ensure we come out on top the next time.

We rehearse how we'll face upcoming events that make us feel fearful. We rehearse past experiences, reliving the way they actually occurred, or re-creating ways we wish they had happened.

Most of us spend more time rehearsing than we realize. And sometimes, we create scenarios and interactions that are far from reality. But they've become very real to us—we believe they're real because we've rehearsed them again and again.

Developing Your Vision for Change

The brain's ability to change is greatest in childhood and adolescence. But change as an adult is still very possible.

Research has debunked the belief that brainpower decreases with age. Knowledge, intelligence, and abilities can be acquired even into old age!

There is a new science called neuroplasticity that focuses on neuro cells. It shows that the brain has the ability to add new nerve cells, change the way its regions communicate, and even rewire or replace some of its parts, remapping message pathways. This can occur, to some degree, throughout our lives.[7] We just have to follow the right methods.

The Bible records that "the LORD saw how great man's wickedness on the earth had become, and that *every inclination of the thoughts of his heart* was only evil all the time" (Gen. 6:5 NIV, emphasis added).

Centuries later, the apostle Paul was still stating the same problem: "Although they knew God, they neither glorified him as God nor gave thanks to him, but *their thinking became futile and their foolish hearts were darkened*" (Rom. 1:21 NIV, emphasis added). Wrong thinking is really a sin problem.

In order to change our thinking and self-talk, we need a vision. You may call it a goal. It involves identifying the way you want your thinking to be. It involves creating a new pattern of thinking and new phrases. But it's more than that.

In *Living above the Level of Mediocrity*, Chuck Swindoll describes what developing a vision really entails:

> Vision is the ability to see God's presence, to perceive God's power, to focus on God's plan, in spite of the obstacles. . . . Vision is the ability to see above and beyond the majority. Vision is perception—reading the presence and power of God into one's circumstances. I sometimes think of vision as looking at life through the lens of God's eyes, seeing situations as He sees them. Too often we see things not as they are, but as we are. Think about that. Vision has to do with looking at life with a divine perspective, reading the scene with God in clear focus.
>
> Whoever wants to live differently in "the system" must correct his or her vision.[8]

Scripture tells us that our minds need to be changed before we can see with God's eyes: "Do not be conformed to this world . . . but be transformed (changed) by the [entire] renewal of your mind [by its new ideals and its new attitude], so that you may prove [for yourselves] what is the good and acceptable and perfect will of God, even the thing which is good and acceptable and perfect" (Rom. 12:2 AMP).

Developing a vision can have powerful effects. As I counseled Trent, he shared with me his vision. He said, "I began to envision not being a person with a load of negative thoughts anymore. I prayed and committed my thought life to God. I actually wrote out in advance new phrases, statements I wanted to make, practiced saying them out loud, prayed about the change . . . and in time I saw a difference. The hardest part was being consistent and establishing a new track record of thinking. But I saw the old pattern diminish and the new increase."

Before you read any more, consider this question. Answer as honestly as you can. It's important.

Do you really believe that you'll be able to change your old thinking pattern? Do you see yourself being different in the future? Think about it for a moment. To help you decide, use the following graph. Place an X along each line that shows where you are right now.

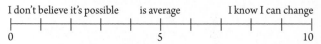

Now indicate where you would like to be:

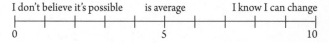

What do your answers on each of the charts indicate about your self-talk? That's an important question.

If you marked the lines between "I don't believe it's possible," and "My hope for changing is average," you may need to override your feelings with the truth of God's Word and his power in your life. Had you considered thinking and praising God, even now, for who you are going to become?

We don't have to wait until after the fact to do this. We can praise and thank him before the change occurs. Strange thought? Perhaps. But think about it in this way.

It's good to start on your path toward change by praising God for who he is, as a response to his love, his goodness, his faithfulness, and his unbelievable concern for each one of us. If we learn to praise God in difficult times, we can recognize his sovereignty and his capacity. In praising God, we are making a transfer—giving trust and dependence to him, rather than trusting and depending upon our own efforts and abilities. He's the one who's involved in your new mind and thoughts.

> Praising God in advance of a solution is an act of faith, a way of saying, I don't know the outcome, but I am willing to trust.

When any of us rejoice in the Lord, it's not necessarily because we feel like it. You can't rely on your feelings. They can come from toxic thoughts.

Rejoicing is an act of our will, a commitment. When we rejoice in the Lord, we begin to see life from another point of view. Praise is the means of gaining a new perspective and new guidance for changing our lives.

Praising God in advance of a solution is an act of faith, a way of saying, I don't know the outcome, but I am willing to trust.

I sometimes ask a person I'm counseling to read aloud this paragraph from Lloyd John Ogilvie's *God's Will in Your Life*:

Praising the Lord makes us willing and releases our imaginations to be used by Him to form the picture of what He is seeking to accomplish. A resistant attitude will make us very uncreative and lacking in adventuresome vision in the use of our capacity of imagination. God wants to use our imagination in the painting of the picture of what He is leading us to dare to hope for and expect. We become what we envision under the Spirit's guidance. That's why our own image of ourselves, other people, our goals, and our projects all need the inspiration of our imagination. However, until the Holy Spirit begins His work releasing it, our will keeps our imagination stunted and immature.[9]

Praise makes a difference because it is an act of relinquishment. It allows God to help us get ready for the next step.

I'm not suggesting you just praise when you hit a crisis in life. I'm suggesting that you develop a consistent pattern of praise. Praising means that we thank him for the fact that the answer is coming, and we'll wait for it. In this case, the answer is the success in changing our self-talk. We know we can expect change, especially those of us who are new creations in Christ.

It's important to remember that, as much as we want to change, we're powerless to do so in our own strength, solely relying on our own efforts. Our minds are bound by the law of sin and death. Without God's help, we cannot change ourselves, no matter how hard we try.

In *Seeing in the Dark*, Gary Kinnaman and Richard Jacobs wrote:

I am compelled to bow down to the idols in the chambers of my imagery. Only by dying to self (putting "me" under the cross) and allowing the Holy Spirit to empower me (hold me up) can I change my old pattern of thinking.

Only with the help and power of the Holy Spirit will I be able to think the thoughts that will change my life. The apostle Paul knew this well. See what he says in Galatians 5:16–18:

> I say, live by the Spirit, and you will not gratify the desires of the sinful nature. For the sinful nature desires what is contrary to the Spirit, and the Spirit what is contrary to the sinful nature. They are in conflict with each other, so that you do not do what you want [I am powerless]. But if you are led by the Spirit, you are not under the law [the futility of human effort].[10]

Only in a personal relationship with Jesus Christ, along with the teaching of God's Word and the ministry of the Holy Spirit, can we experience the greatest and most lasting change in our life. As we read in 2 Timothy 3:16–17, "Every Scripture is God-breathed (given by His inspiration) and profitable for instruction, for reproof and conviction of sin, for correction of error and discipline in obedience, [and] for training in righteousness (in holy living, in conformity to God's will in thought, purpose, and action), so that the man of God may be complete and proficient, well fitted and thoroughly equipped for every good work" (AMP).

And in Hebrews 4:12, we see, "For the Word that God speaks is alive and full of power [making it active, operative, energizing, and effective]; it is sharper than any two-edged sword, penetrating to the dividing line of the breath of life (soul) and [the immortal] spirit, and of joints and marrow [of the deepest parts of our nature], exposing and sifting and analyzing and judging the very thoughts and purposes of the heart" (AMP).

Read these verses out loud every day for a month, allowing them to sink into your *heart* and *mind*. They will be yours for life.

Change will happen when we practice and rehearse, but we need to be consistent in doing our part.

Reflect and Remember

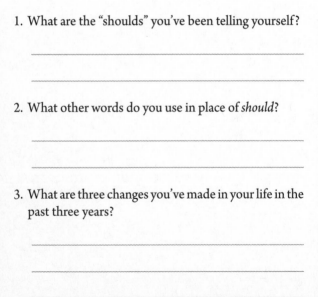

1. What are the "shoulds" you've been telling yourself?

   _____

   _____

2. What other words do you use in place of *should*?

   _____

   _____

3. What are three changes you've made in your life in the past three years?

   _____

   _____

   _____

4. Complete this sentence: I will deliberately practice changing my self-talk by . . .

_____

_____

5. Identify three praises you have for God at this time:

_____

_____

_____

_____

Knocking Out
Toxic Self-Talk . . . for Good!

Matt was a specialist with the fire department. He worked with hazardous materials and was called in whenever there was a dangerous situation.

Some of his work involved containing toxic materials. Other men in the department started out working with these materials, but either dropped out or made a mistake and suffered burns.

One day, Matt was interviewed after successfully containing a dangerous spill. He was asked how he was able to be so successful in his dangerous work. His response was not what was expected. He told the interviewer this: At each event where he was expected to take charge, there were two possible toxic spills. One was the active spill he'd been called to contain—that was reality. The other possible toxic spill would be in his own mind.

If his thoughts were negative, fearful, and focused on the worst possible outcome, he was more likely to make a mistake, he admitted. But if he focused on what he knew as the correct procedures, and was cautious, and reminded himself of what he'd done before and all he knew about his job, he was more likely to be successful . . . and safe. His final remark: "It all depends on what goes on in my mind."

By now, you know that much of life is directed by our thoughts. And sometimes we're not even certain if what we believe is true or not.

As Christians we're called to test what we think is the truth. This is why some of our time and effort needs to be given to our thought life. It affects our spiritual life.

We all have false beliefs, some of us more than others. I'm hoping you've already started challenging your false beliefs, replacing them with positive self-talk.

In this chapter, I'm going to give you several more ways to challenge toxic patterns in your thought life.

As we said before, it's possible to change. It also takes work. Expect results, but not instant results. Once again, remember the importance of rehearsal and practice.

Strategies to Neutralize Toxic Thoughts

Let's identify a false belief that has wielded power in your life. Then, using the following simple exercise, let's strip it of its power.

This exercise is far more powerful if you complete it in writing. I suspect you'll quickly discover the difference it will make. I'd like you to commit ten minutes per day to repeating this every day for the next three weeks.

Write a thorough answer to each of the following four questions. I've given you an example of each one.

- What major false belief do I want to eliminate?

  Response: I probably have no chance at getting that job I want.

  _____

  _____

  _____

  _____

  _____

- What evidence can I discover that makes my idea false?

  Response: My résumé shows I'm well qualified. I have interviewed well in the past, and have landed jobs I wanted.

  _____

  _____

  _____

  _____

  _____

- If what I want doesn't occur (getting the job) or the undesirable does happen, what's the worst outcome?

  Response: I will be disappointed, but there will be other opportunities. It won't bring terrible consequences. I still have another job that brings in the money I need to cover my bills. I will be able to handle the disappointment.

  _____

  _____

  _____

  _____

- If what I want doesn't occur, or if the undesirable thing does occur, what satisfying things could I do as an alternative?

  Response: I could focus on working toward advancement at my current job. I could ask the interviewer what I could do to improve my chances in the future. I could use this experience to rely more upon God and seek his will for the right job. I can thank him for closing this door, and trust that it was the best for me at this time.

  _____

  _____

  _____

  _____

Some find it helpful to write these questions on a three-by-five-inch card and carry the card around with them. Whenever their thoughts stray back to a false belief, they take out the card and reread the questions, taking time to answer them carefully—aloud, if possible. That will help reinforce your new pattern of thinking. It may feel strange. But if it works, what do you have to lose?

There are many approaches to handling toxic or negative thoughts. What do you do when you receive the mail each day? If you're like most of us, you sort through it. You may have a pile for magazines, a pile for first-class letters, and a pile for junk mail. That pile gets tossed into the trash.

Many of our thoughts are junk thoughts. Imagine labeling them "junk mail" and tossing them from your mind. As you bring in new healthy and realistic thoughts, consider them your first-class mail.

Here's another strategy: In my house, I have a shredder to dispose of paper I don't want. If you struggle with your thoughts, especially when you're trying to fall asleep, try to imagine them coming out of your head in the form of pieces of paper. Imagine putting them into a shredder and seeing the results destroyed. Catching them as quickly as you can, then "shredding" them before they gain a foothold, helps this process be successful.[1]

> Imagine labeling junk thoughts as "junk mail" and tossing them from your mind.

The following exercise also will help you gain a healthier pattern of thinking. It's a thought-evaluation worksheet, and it can help you uproot false beliefs and replace them with proper, objective beliefs. Try this with one of the negative thoughts that plague you:

Situation	Correct Analysis of the Situation
(Briefly describe the undesirable situation that upsets you.)	(This is done to determine whether the description you have given of your situation is accurate.)
I can't continue working here since I've been passed over for a promotion three times. My husband is constantly pressuring me to quit.	Yes, this is true. I have been passed over for some unknown reason. My husband pressures me every day and I'm tired of it.

Self-talk or inner conversations	Thought challenges and alternative interpretations
(List the specific statements that you tell yourself when you think about this unfair and undesirable situation.)	(This is the time to challenge the statement and list alternative statements that would appropriately describe the meaning of your situation and be in your own best interest to believe.)
1. This is awful.	1. Where's the evidence that this is awful? This is disappointing but it isn't the end of the world. I've handled other disappointments before. I may discover the reason for being passed over and be able to correct it.
2. This is totally unfair to not be promoted.	2. What's unfair about this? That depends on how I interpret it. Fairness is not the issue here.
3. My husband is just thinking about himself and how much money I can bring home.	3. How do I know that my husband is thinking just about himself? That's mind reading. Have I asked him why I should quit? He may have some insights I don't have.

Self-talk or inner conversations	Thought challenges and alternative interpretations
4. If I quit, I'm not sure I'd get any recommendations and I couldn't get as good a job.	4. How do I know I won't get a recommendation? I'm quite good at my job, and people like me. There's no evidence that I couldn't get a better job.

Exposing Assumptions That Heighten Negative Self-Talk

False assumptions stimulate much of our negative self-talk. Identifying them—and their consequences—can bring about change.

Kathy complained during counseling, "I really have to do what others expect me to do." This unrealistic assumption left her feeling pressured and manipulated.

After completing the following exercise, she saw the cost of following that assumption.

Advantages of believing this and acting upon it	Disadvantages of believing this and acting upon it
1. If I can meet other people's expectations, I feel like I'm in control. I like this. It feels good.	1. When I do this, I sometimes compromise. I do things that I really don't want to do. They're not the best for me.
2. I feel secure when I please others.	2. When I do what others want me to do, no matter what, I end up never knowing if others like me just for who I am. I end up being their slave, doing things for them in order to ensure I'm accepted.

Advantages of believing this and acting upon it	Disadvantages of believing this and acting upon it
3. I don't have to figure things out for myself since I depend on others telling me what to do.	3. Wow. This really lets others control me. I give them power over me. I'm not really in control.
4. I don't have to be concerned about people not liking me or accepting me.	4. But do they really like me for me? How do I know that? Always being the good guy limits me. If I do what I want to do, what will they think? I live in fear of their rejection!
5. I don't have much conflict in my life, because I'm such a people pleaser.	5. Sometimes people do disapprove of me, in spite of my trying to please them, and then I feel rotten. *I can't do anything right* is my thought.

What are three assumptions or beliefs you have?

_____

_____

_____

_____

_____

_____

_____

_____

Pleasing Others Doesn't Have to Be Your Goal

Many people who suffer with toxic thinking mistakenly believe things will be better if they try to please others all the time. If you feel that way, these misbeliefs may sound familiar:

- The way to be liked is to be what other people want me to be and do what is most pleasing to them.
- It is more Christian to please other people than to please myself.
- Others have the right to judge my actions. It's wrong and un-Christian to think my own needs are important, when compared to the needs of others.
- It's wrong to not put aside my own wants in order to please friends and family.
- Pleasing others is an insurance policy that guarantees people will be nice to me in return. When I'm in need, they'll forget their own needs and help me, as I helped them.
- When other people are displeased with me, it's impossible for me to get a moment's peace or happiness.
- Approval from everyone else is absolutely necessary to my feelings of well-being and peace of mind. God is most pleased when everyone else is approving of me.
- Pleasing others, and doing what they expect of me, is the only way to win friends.

Remember Matt, the fireman? He'd say this is toxic thinking. That's because it's impossible to please others all the time. And that kind of thinking gives others control of our lives, causing us to live in bondage. That's not the way Scripture instructs us to live.

It's far healthier to train yourself to challenge these beliefs with thoughts that are positive, balanced, and healthy, such as:

- It's not necessary to be liked by everyone.
- I don't have to earn anyone's approval or acceptance to be a person of worth.
- I am a child of God. I am deeply loved by him, and I have been forgiven by him; therefore I am acceptable. I accept myself.
- My needs and wants are as important as other people's.
- Rejection is not terrible. It may be a bit unpleasant, but it's not the worst thing that can happen.
- Not being approved or accepted is not awful. It may not be desirable, but it does not have tragic consequences.
- If somebody doesn't like me, I can live with it. I don't have to work feverishly to get any person to like me.
- I can conquer my bad feelings by distinguishing the truth from misbelief.
- It is a misbelief that I must please other people and be approved by them.
- Jesus died on the cross for me so that I can be free from the misbelief that other people decide my value.

Saying "No More!" to Negative Thinking

Yet another approach to banishing toxic thinking is called "So *WHAT* if it happens!"

What negative thought worries you? Maybe you tend to fret about the possibility of losing your job.

Okay, let's assume it actually might happen. First of all, what are the chances? Let's give it a mathematical value. Is your company laying off 10 percent of the workforce? So let's say you have a one-in-ten chance of receiving the pink slip you dread.

Now, assuming it happens, is it that terrible? Is it really a catastrophe? Do you have savings? Do you have family or friends who could help you while you look for a new job? Would they really let you starve, or become homeless? Probably not.

Ask yourself, Do I really have the ability to keep this from happening? Can I prevent it? If not, worrying really doesn't help.

Ask yourself, Am I incapable of handling it? Where's the evidence for that? What other crises have I experienced in my life? How have I handled those? It's empowering to talk yourself through the worst.

Another method that works well in kicking out toxic thinking—including worry, depression, and anger—is a step-by-step approach suggested by Archibald Hart.

But before I describe this, I want to emphasize that it's important to make each step a matter of prayer. Ask for strength, guidance, and the ability to stay focused on each. Sometimes it's helpful to ask a friend to be a support or a sponsor of sorts to encourage you in the process. It also helps to keep a notebook or three-by-five-inch cards on which to record your responses during the day.

Your first step is to identify, or "capture," your thoughts. The apostle Paul described taking "captive every thought" in this passage: "For though we live in the world, we do not wage war as the world does. The weapons we fight with are not the weapons of the world. On the contrary, they have divine power to demolish strongholds. We demolish arguments and every pretension that sets itself up against the knowledge of God, and we take captive every thought to make it obedient to Christ" (2 Cor. 10:3–5 NIV).

This first step requires that you go beyond just identifying a thought. You need to begin with an emotion. Whenever you have an emotional reaction, label the emotion no matter what it is, whether it's negative or positive. Write it down.

Each emotion is actually a signal letting you know that something else is going on. Write *why* you are feeling the way you do. You could have more than one reason. (We'll talk more about worry, anger, and depression in upcoming chapters.)

Then ask yourself, What are the thoughts that prompted this emotion? It could have been a series of events or ideas. Try to put the thoughts you had in the sequence in which they occurred. Did your thought bother you, encourage you, hinder your life in some way?

At the end of each day, review what you've written, and note if there's a pattern to your entries. Are there patterns to the thoughts or when they occurred? If you do this for a week, you may find a theme to your thoughts. Once you've identified the patterns, the next step is to evaluate them.

The important question is: Are these thoughts enhancing my life or detracting from it? Write your responses to these questions. Seeing the results will have a more powerful effect on you.

Are your thoughts accurate? It's important to be aware of what your thoughts are, what prompts them, and what their impact is on you and the people around you.

God knows our thoughts better than we do. Sometimes my thoughts puzzle me, confuse me, trouble me, surprise me, or delight me. But what is most important is what God thinks about my thoughts.

As I've said before, it's also important to determine the core issue behind each negative thought. You can ask yourself, Is the thought the issue? Or is there something deeper causing this negative thinking pattern?

You might consider: If I shared this thought with others, what would they say about it? Is there a decision I need to make about this thought's presence?

Now, you're ready to challenge your negative thoughts—in writing. You want to show whether it's true or not. Consider these questions:

- What says it is true?
- Is there a law that says this?
- Why should I believe this?
- Is this a hangover from childish reasoning?
- What is the worst consequence I can expect even if this is true?
- What prevents me from changing this belief?
- Are there ways I can prove or disprove the thought?
- If I take the idea to its extreme, what is its ultimate conclusion?[2]

The next step is changing your thoughts. Repeatedly writing out your answers to these questions with pen and paper—instead of typing them on a computer—and verbalizing them aloud again and again is what will make them stick. You've heard this before.

The final step is thought prevention. This can be the most difficult step. Sometimes, trying to keep the thought from occurring only serves to make it stronger and more likely to rear its ugly head.

It's like if I asked you *not* to think of the color red. See? You're thinking of the color red, right?

If the thought occurs often because of your years of producing it, accept it and use the previous steps.[3]

This may be a lot to remember. That's why it's important to journal these activities and commit to practicing them.

Think of the material you've been learning in this way. You're a prospector searching for gold. You've just discovered a vein of riches, but it's embedded in rock. Now, it's up to you to dig it out. Doing so will make you wealthy.

What you've read can lie dormant on these pages. Or the strategies can change your thinking . . . and your life. It's up to you, but not entirely. God is working in your life as well, guiding and strengthening you.

Change can happen.

Finding the Motivation to Push On

One of the best ways to eradicate a bad habit is to establish a new one that competes with the bad one. If the newly established good habit is put into practice repeatedly over the old, the old habit gradually will fade away. But we have to work diligently at replacing our bad habits with good ones. The bad ones have a foothold that must be dislodged.

Recently a crane discovered a small pond I have in my backyard. In the pond are minnows, a few bluegill, an albino catfish, two frogs, and two turtles. This pond provides me with a great deal of relaxation and enjoyment. And I didn't like the crane coming and standing in my pond—I knew what he'd do to the wildlife.

To discourage the newcomer, I opened the door and let my dogs rush out to chase him away. Off he flew.

I assumed he was gone for good. He wasn't. He perched in the branches of a tree . . . and waited. As soon as we went inside, he fluttered back down to the water's edge, intent on a morning meal.

We rushed outside again, and again he took off. And yet again, he returned when we left our post. The pattern repeated itself until he finally gave up and flew away.

I shared this story with Charlene in her counseling session. "I can relate to that," she said. "It's just what happens when I try to get rid of my negative thoughts. As soon as I come in with some better ones, they leave. But the minute I relax and let down, there they are again. They're really ingrained, aren't they?"

Creating a good habit requires a strong motivation for change. Simply having a desire for self-improvement isn't enough. Knowing what to do to create the new habit helps. But that, by itself, won't get the job done, as every unsuccessful New Year's resolution maker will attest. We all know what we *should* do, but that doesn't mean we'll do it.

It's vital to fuel your motivation. How? Working in a group can provide the best incentive.

Overwhelming research in the field of weight loss has shown that the key to losing weight and keeping it off lies in having group support.[4] If you can persuade someone else to work with you in your quest to banish negative thinking, perhaps a friend or spouse, you're likely to find it far easier to keep up your motivation. Regular contact with others can encourage you, instruct you, help you deal with failure, and enable you to avoid mistakes.

You'll also protect your motivation if you give yourself time to change. Nothing kills motivation like impatience. It is a well-known fact that to give up a substance like sugar or caffeine, your body takes twenty-one days to adjust. Before that time has passed, the body treats the change as an intruder.

> You'll also protect your motivation if you give yourself time to change. Nothing kills motivation like impatience.

Only after three weeks will your body accept the change as natural. The body thrives on stability. It resists change as much as possible, and adapts to new situations slowly.

The twenty-one-day rule applies to most changes we want to make. When you've introduced a new habit or stopped an old one, be sure to be persistent in the new behavior for at least twenty-one days. Don't expect a new habit to feel natural right away. Some habits might take twice as long to really stick. So be patient.

You need to adopt the attitude of the marathon runner, not the impulsive sprinter. Long-distance runners are patient and unhurried. They know how to pace themselves. Think about the fable of the tortoise and the hare. The tortoise won because he had the right attitude. He had vision. He was in for the long haul.

Motivation survives best if you're flexible, and if you build in some room for failure. Rigid programs of change fizzle because of their inflexibility.

Many who begin a diet set themselves up for failure because of rigid standards or expectations that are too high.

A healthy mind is a mind that can tolerate setbacks and then bounce back.[5]

Now that you've completed this chapter, you've learned several options for banishing negative thinking and building the habit of replacing toxic thoughts with positive ones. Whichever method you choose, stick with it long enough to give it time to work. Believe that it can. And remember the scriptural passages that promise that you can get your thinking right, with God's help. God's Word *will* work and it *will* make the difference, as you work toward changing your thought life.

Reflect and Remember

1. Complete this sentence: I commit to complete my thought-evaluation form by this date . . .

   _____

2. List three negative assumptions or beliefs you want to eliminate:

   _____

   _____

   _____

3. Which method will you use for three weeks, in order to develop the habit of thinking more positively?

   _____

   _____

4. Who are the people in your life who could help you in changing your thought life?

_____

_____

5. Return to the previous chapters and make a list of all the Scriptures we've used up to this point:

_____

_____

_____

_____

_____

_____

_____

_____

Disarming Toxic Weapons
in Your Marriage

Alaska, 1988. Prince William Sound. The *Exxon Valdez*.

These words remind us of one of our country's worst environmental disasters. The giant oil tanker spewed 11 million gallons of crude oil into pristine waters, contaminating more than 1,200 miles of shoreline. The tragedy killed 1,000 sea otters and more than 100,000 birds, including 150 bald eagles. People who made their living in the fishing industry lost more than $100 billion combined. The aftermath of that oil spill is still with us more than twenty-two years later.

Toxic materials contaminate our cities too. Chemicals thoughtlessly dumped into landfills years ago now haunt us. Toxic fumes seep into homes built over these landfills. Families have been uprooted, as entire communities have evacuated to avoid the danger of toxicity.

On an international scale, superpowers argue about the stockpile of nuclear weapons posing imminent danger to the entire world.

Just as our world has problems with dangerous contamination, toxicity, and weapons, so do our marriages.

Thousands of couples walk the aisle each year. They move toward the pastor, eagerly awaiting the sharing of vows and the pronouncement, "You are now man and wife." The new life, anticipated with romantic dreams of blissful, forever-togetherness has begun.

Now, fast-forward five years, and what do you find? Some couples are moving forward, having made adjustments and having grown together. Others are shattered, struggling, fighting, maybe even divorced.

What makes the difference? In many cases their thoughts, which used to be positive about each other and their relationship, have turned negative. Destructive beliefs and labels wave angrily in the wind. Each one is judged and sentenced in the other's mind. Allowances for differences have fallen by the wayside, replaced by thoughts of condemnation. What started out as hopeful beliefs for the future have twisted into despair. Each partner nurses wounds inflicted by the one they love.

Words as Weapons

In marriages filled with hurt, spouses often poison and wound each other with the words they use. And often, they learned to speak this way by watching their own parents.

You may have grown up with parents who used words as weapons, and you vowed not to do the same. But we tend to repeat familial patterns—unless we become the one to break the pattern and develop new habits of communication that reflect the presence of Jesus Christ. No matter how bad your marriage has become, such a change *is* possible!

What we have to eliminate are the toxic weapons we form against each other—those cruel, caustic, bitter, degrading, and judgmental words we use to inflict hurt. They contaminate, wound, poison, and destroy others emotionally.

Our words are often launched as verbal missiles to attack others' behavior, appearance, intelligence, competence, or value as a person.

In James 3:8–10, the writer recognizes the potentially toxic nature of the words we speak: "The human tongue can be tamed by no man. It

> **What we have to eliminate are the toxic weapons we form against each other.**

is a restless (undisciplined, irreconcilable) evil, full of deadly poison. With it we bless the Lord and Father, and with it we curse men who were made in God's likeness! Out of the same mouth come forth blessing and cursing. These things, my brethren, ought not to be so" (AMP).

Words bruise and batter on the inside like physical blows bruise and lacerate the skin. That's why we call the use of these words "verbal abuse." We're often unaware of the damage our words cause because we can't see the inner cuts and bruises.

But even when verbal assault stops, the emotional damage continues within the victim.

Toxic words in marriages come from toxic thoughts.

Removing Toxic Thoughts from Your Marriage

Slander is the utterance in the presence of another person of a false statement or statements, damaging to a third person's character or reputation.[1] Many of our thoughts about one another fall into that category. And God knows them all.

Many spouses commit slander in their minds. Some of those thoughts are closer to character assassination, rather than character adoration. And this style of thinking generates both conflict and distance in the marriage relationship.

Couples who have growing, fulfilling marriages have thought lives that are positive and healthy. What happens between the couples is a reflection of the inner workings of each person's mind and heart.

Many, however, struggle with defeatist beliefs, thoughts such as: Our marriage will never improve, or, He won't ever change, or, She just doesn't really love me.

But as people work at challenging these negative beliefs about their spouse and their marriage, they *can* become positive in their thinking. They can change—and that change can transform their spouse, and their marriage as well.

After such promising beginnings, where do negative thoughts and marital problems begin? Why can't people get along and love one another? People often ask, "What's the main issue?"

Quite simply, it all goes back to the fall of man—sin.

The world still reaps the results of or damage from original sin in the ways we behave, feel, and think. Our thoughts are where sin takes root. God pointed this out early in Genesis. Remember the passage we considered earlier: "Then the LORD saw that the wickedness of man was great on the earth, and that every intent of the thoughts of his heart was only evil continually" (Gen. 6:5 NASB). In other versions of the Bible, the word *thoughts* is translated *imagination*. Again, it is in our minds where sin begins.

I've never been in a hurricane, and I never want to be. The tremendous force of the violent, swirling winds devastates everything in its path, leaving behind a trail of destruction.

However, within a hurricane is the eye of the storm—a place of such calm, you wouldn't even suspect the fury raging around the perimeter. While it is calm, it's still connected to the intense, violent winds that stem outward from the core.

Consider these storms that form out of one spouse's negative thinking:

1. A husband comes home from work early and greets his wife with a hug and kiss. But in return she becomes angry and glares at him. Why?
2. A wife returns her husband's overdue books to the library, and he becomes annoyed at her for doing so. Why?
3. A husband brags about his wife's cooking to a number of friends, and she becomes furious at him for doing so. Why?

In each case, the spouse's positive action brings an unexpected reaction from his or her spouse. Appreciation would be the expected reaction. And yet, anger was aroused. What happened?

Let's go back and look at the thoughts each spouse had in response to the positive overture.

In the case of the wife whose husband came home early, she thought, Why did he come home now? Is he checking up on me? If there's anything undone, he'll think I wasn't staying busy. I don't need the criticism!

The husband with the overdue library books thought, I was going to take those back. I'm capable of doing that. She's trying to point out that I'm not responsible. She doesn't trust me to follow through, so she's going to jump in and do it herself!

The wife who was praised for her cooking thought, He never praises me that much at home. He's just using me to get attention for himself from his friends. He probably wants me to compliment him on something now. I wonder what they think about me now?

In each case, negative thoughts just popped into their minds, and they reacted angrily.

Ever happened to you? Probably. But why?

Perhaps your thought was based on a past experience, or maybe you were having a difficult day. In each case, regardless of the intent and purpose of the spouse who did something positive, the angry reaction might limit a positive overture another time, and thus create a cycle of negativity.

Loveless Labels

Negative thoughts don't paint an accurate picture of your spouse. They are limited, biased, and slanted in one direction.

In his book *The Forgiving Marriage*, Paul Coleman points out that labeling your spouse with negative titles, such as callous, selfish, controlling, insensitive, manipulative, unbending, crazy, and so on, creates a one-sided depiction of your spouse.[2]

More important, thoughts and labels interfere with one of the ingredients most essential for a marriage to change, progress, and move forward—forgiveness. Can you forgive a person after you've thought of or labeled him or her negatively?

Labels are a convenient way of expressing dissatisfaction and anger. When we label someone in our minds, we assign them to a restrictive box, which doesn't allow exceptions or positives to exist. We can do this to ourselves, as well as to others. The result is the same: Labeling *anyone* limits our perception of them and their abilities. And frequently, labels of others are used to cover our own tendencies.

Labels are false absolutes. They are developed to describe those who are different, and to keep us from having to think. Labels also make it easier to justify what we think or how we behave.

If we used our minds constructively, we would be able to see both sides of a person. Labels limit our understanding of what occurs in a marriage—we see the label as the cause of the problem. Why look elsewhere?

Labels keep us from looking at our part in the problem. We use labels to avoid looking in the mirror, for fear of what we will see in the reflection. When you treat your spouse as if he or she is a certain way and possesses a particular quality, he or she may begin to act that way. Our negative thoughts and labels often become self-fulfilling prophecies. We end up cultivating exactly what we don't want to grow.

For example, if a spouse is overly negative and critical, he or she may behave in a defensive or angry manner. That may cause the other to be negative and critical as well. Then the first spouse feels justified in his or her beliefs.

Do you and your spouse label each other? Are the labels positive and motivating, or negative and debilitating? Are they attached to descriptions such as "always" or "never"?

If you do label your spouse, consider correcting the label and, in your heart and mind, give him or her an opportunity to be different.

Our negative, labeling thoughts can put a damper on an otherwise enjoyable occasion. But derailing those labels can stop the downhill slide.

Consider June and her husband, Frank. After they went to a movie, Frank suggested they walk down to a restaurant for a piece of pie. Look inside their minds as the conversation continued:

June's first thought was, Oh boy. He knows I've been trying to diet and lose weight. He's just thinking of himself as usual. You'd think he'd remember something as important as that.

She responds with an exasperated "No, I'd rather just go home."

Frank thinks, Now what's wrong with her? We had a great time, and now she's getting all bent out of shape. She sure goes up and down with her emotions. "Fine," he says, "just forget it."

They walk to the car in silence. But they both begin to recognize how their thoughts fed the way they responded to each other. So during their silence, each one silently challenges those destructive thoughts.

June begins to think, Well, maybe he just didn't think about it. After all, he's not the one on a diet, I am. And he's probably hungry. I could have a cup of decaf.

Feeling remorseful, she thinks, I guess I would prefer to go home and get some sleep. I've been overworked this month. I guess I must have snapped at him, and I didn't need to. His request was innocent enough.

Meanwhile, Frank tells himself, June really has been pushing it at work recently. And it's 10:30. Maybe she's tired and wants to go home.

He reassures himself, We've worked out other disagreements. Surely this is no big deal.

June's voice breaks through his thoughts: "I didn't need to snap at you. I guess I was thinking about myself a bit too much. I was looking forward to getting some rest. But you're probably hungry."

Frank sighs in relief: "I appreciate your clarifying that; I know you've been working a lot. And I just remembered you're watching what you eat. Eating pie in front of you might make you drool. And *that* would be embarrassing for both of us."

With that comment, they both laugh, thankful to have turned things around.

Exorcising Emotional Ghosts

Sometimes we can't explain why we react the way we do. In a counseling session, Mark asked in frustration, as he described the way he responded bitterly toward his wife, without provocation, "Why do I respond in this way? I don't understand why my mind goes down that path. Sometimes I feel haunted!"

Some people actually do refer to these unexpectedly hostile responses as "emotional ghosts." In their book *Why Can't You Read My Mind?* Jeffrey Bernstein and Susan Magee describe it this way:

> Partners who have unresolved "emotional ghosts" from their past are particularly at risk for toxic thinking. I can easily argue that we all have some emotional ghosts from our pasts. But the more important point is the extent to which they still haunt you. For many people, childhood was not a bed of roses. If family problems (such as emotional or physical abandonment, addictions, financial stress, mental illness, body-image problems, peer difficulties, learning disabilities, and many other types of issues) are not worked through and understood as children and teens, they can predispose adults to use toxic thought patterns toward their parents.[3]

Some emotional ghosts come from conditional love we experienced as children—receiving love only when we behaved well, and being rejected when we didn't.

Unfortunately, in many cases, some end up selecting a marriage partner who responds to them as their parents did. Why? It's what we know best, but it's not the best for us. It's like a moth being drawn to a flame. We all like to think we're in charge of our lives, but many find their present life dictated by unresolved issues of the past.

These emotional ghosts, also known as "baggage," come from many sources. It could be experiences with peers that were painful. It could be bad experiences within friendships or romantic relationships.

These emotional ghosts exercise influence by causing us to hear remembered statements over and over again:

You're so inept.

I can't believe you did something so stupid.

You won't amount to anything.

Blew it again, huh?

Why try? You'll never make it.

No one will ever listen to you.

You should do better.

When you hear a toxic statement enough, no one else needs to say it anymore. You pick it up and continue voicing it to yourself, making it part of who you are, even though it's not true. But why would anyone want to make these statements to themselves?

These emotional ghosts come from thoughts that are stored in your memory banks. You'll remember that each experience leaves a residue that shapes our actions and emotions.

> Emotional ghosts come from thoughts that are stored in your memory banks.

We've said this before, but it may still be a new thought or concept for you. It may take time to really sink in. But it's important to become more aware of the possible presence of emotional ghosts, what they say and how this impacts you, and how your thoughts reflect their presence. If you're experiencing some type of a problem in your relationships, consider the possibility of a connection with an emotional ghost.

Listen to those messages about yourself from your past. What are they saying? Who's saying them? In *A Dad-Shaped Hole in My Heart*, I quoted Jenny, who described her emotional ghosts in this way:

> We have movies today about the whisperer—*The Horse Whisperer, The Dog Whisperer, The Ghost Whisperer*. Well, they need to make another movie: *The Parent Whisperer*. I can hear them right inside my head—I hear them when I dress my daughter, when I try something new, when I want to eat that dessert, when I want to spend a large amount of money. Oh, no one else can hear her, but I can. And it's strange: They didn't always say it verbally; it was the way mom or dad looked at me. I guess I've transcribed that into an audible whisper.
>
> My parents live in my head. They sit up there and program what I think, what I say, and what I do. I'd like to find the disconnect button and then give an eviction notice.
>
> I received the ultimate insult the other day from my husband. I was correcting my daughter about something and he said, "Jenny, you sound just like your mother!" I was shocked. I stopped and looked at him, fuming. And probably because he was right! It's not just what I say outwardly. It's what I'm saying to myself.[4]

Many messages you may hear in your parents' voices are actually "rules" they taught you. Some are good, others not so good—some are healthy, and others are not so healthy.

Often, they come in the form of "shoulds" and "oughts." Your parents likely taught you when to engage in certain activities; what to say in certain situations; even how to arrange your own home.

Some of those rules reflected your parents' fears. Some were there to protect you. Others were given in the hope that you would experience the best in life.

Some rules were handed down from your grandparents. You may be able to identify the times and places you first heard certain rules. Some were heard again and again, so it's no wonder they found a place in your belief system—you repeated these to yourself.

From parents you might have learned:

- Which subjects should be discussed, and which were off-limits.
- When it was appropriate to discuss certain subjects and when it was not.
- With whom to associate and whom to avoid.
- What your family would or wouldn't do.
- How you were supposed to act around the opposite sex.
- How you were supposed to feel about school.
- How you were supposed to feel about work.
- How you were supposed to feel about yourself.
- The way you should act at certain functions.

All of these can affect your marital relationship.

What are your emotional ghosts, and how do they affect you and your spouse? Is your past interfering with your marital relationship? The first step in correcting that is clearly identifying a problem you're having in your marriage relationship.

_____

_____

_____

_____

_____

Why do you think this problem exists? How do you usually explain it to yourself?

_____

_____

_____

_____

_____

What event from your past relates to this current issue? What thoughts connect the two?

_____

_____

_____

_____

Describe how what happened in the past impacts you. How did it hurt you, affect your beliefs, etc.?

_____

_____

_____

_____

Has this emotional ghost affected any other relationships prior to this current one? Describe how.

_____

_____

_____

_____

We all struggle with emotional ghosts. Scripture speaks of this as the "old self" (Rom. 6:6 NASB). The old self was programmed by early experiences. And even before our lives began, we were affected by the fall of man. Thus, we begin life with a mind that has a propensity toward negative thinking, worry, fear, guilt, and remembering experiences that would be better off relinquished.

Even after we become believers, the residue—the emotional ghosts—of old thinking remains and exercises influence through our will, our emotions, our thoughts, and our behavior.[5]

Because the focus of this book is on changing your present thoughts, I'm not going to devote much time to the past. But if your past haunts you and damages your relationships, I would recommend that you read my books *Making Peace with Your Past* and *Healing Grace for Broken Relationships*.

Why Negative Thoughts about Your Marriage Must Go

Whenever your spouse does something that's neutral—neither overtly positive or negative—you can choose to react with a negative interpretation, an assumption, suspicion of intent, or guarded and defensive manner. On the other hand, you have the choice to respond at face value to what was said or done, give the benefit of the doubt, see it as a positive step, and then show appreciation.

Of these two choices, the Bible would point to the latter as the correct response. First Corinthians 13:7 says, "Love . . . is ever ready to believe the best of every person" (AMP).

Will you let your negative thoughts generate anger toward your spouse? The choice is yours.

One way to keep love alive and moving in a positive direction in your relationship is to have full awareness of your thoughts and beliefs toward your spouse. When facing a problem or negative situation in your marriage, first look at your own thoughts. There's a good chance that by turning around your negative thoughts, you'll find your solution. You and your spouse will appreciate the resulting peace.

Negative thoughts can kill the love in a marriage. They can escalate perceptions so much so that a neutral behavior can be seen as negative.

Sadly, it's often the very qualities that attract two people to each other that later are seen by each other as negative. It's not that the attributes that each enjoyed or admired have disappeared. They're still there.

But if self-talk about a spouse tends to be negative, it can seep into and affect one's perception even of the qualities once thought attractive.

Jim and Janice had been married for eight years. In many ways, they were quite different from each other. But that was part of the attraction. Janice was attracted to Jim's easygoing and accepting personality. He was a fun-loving guy. He had his own business and was always "just one step" away from making it big.

Jim was drawn to the way Janice, a competent and somewhat assertive attorney, stayed in control of her life and didn't let others push her around.

But eight years into their marriage, what initially attracted them to each other had become sources of irritation. They'd hung ugly labels on each other.

Janice now saw Jim as "lazy, irresponsible, and passive." To Jim, Janice now seemed "controlling, critical, and overbearing."

Why the change? In large part, their self-talk was to blame. As Jim's business failed to grow, Janice encouraged him to put in more time and effort. Jim saw this as pressure. He labeled her as nagging and controlling, and became withdrawn and passive.

Janice saw this as lazy. She became pushy and critical. Jim became even more resentful and unmotivated.

It's interesting that their original perceptions about each other had changed so much. Fortunately, with some work, they realized what their negative self-talk about each other had done to their relationship.

Jim's Self-Talk

Negative Label	New, Positive Label
She's controlling.	She's actually decisive, gets a lot done, contributes to family income.
She's critical.	She's sharp and decisive; she's very successful; she doesn't intend to hurt me.

Janice's Self-Talk

Negative Label	New, Positive Label
He's lazy.	He's laid-back, easygoing.
He makes a joke out of everything. He's not serious enough.	He's got a great sense of humor. He can always make me laugh when I'm feeling down.

When Jim and Janice learned to reframe their self-talk about each other in this way, the negative labels they'd fumed about lost their sting.[6] Their relationship grew again.

Storms are a part of life. We have no control over the rain, tornadoes, or hurricanes. And they can be destructive.

Storms of the mind can be just as destructive. But these, we can control. It's a choice. Monitor your thoughts. If they build your relationships, keep them. In fact, feed them!

If they don't add something positive to a relationship, evict them. Replace them with thoughts that are positive. This can make all the difference.

Reflect and Remember

Are you fully aware of your thoughts about your marriage and your spouse? Take a few minutes and write out your thoughts. It will help you determine whether your thoughts promote or hinder growth in your marriage.

1. My positive thoughts about my spouse are:

_____

_____

_____

_____

2. My negative thoughts about my spouse are:

_____

_____

_____

_____

3. Beliefs I have that help my marriage grow are:

_____

_____

_____

_____

4. Beliefs I have that keep my marriage from growing are:

_____

_____

_____

_____

5. What I will do to build my marriage is:

_____

_____

_____

_____

9

Dousing "Hot" Thoughts

Tina could be a real leader in her company at times. She came up with creative ideas that boosted productivity and sales, and always seemed to be two steps ahead of her co-workers. But sometimes, as she talked to people, she sounded pushy, aggressive, impatient, even a bit angry.

One day, her supervisor, Bill, took her aside.

"Do you know the difference between 'hot thoughts' and 'cold thoughts'?" he asked.

For once, Tina was speechless. She just shook her head.

"Well," he began, "sometimes our thoughts are hot—they're angry, critical, or blaming. Sometimes they seem to try to read others' minds. And when we think hot thoughts, they influence what we say."

He paused, to let his words sink in.

"Just something to think about," he said gently, as he turned to walk away.

Tina did think about it. Suddenly, she began to realize how many people she'd probably offended with the words that spewed out after hot thoughts. Being a Christian, she sought guidance in Scripture, and eventually learned to douse her hot thoughts.

Relationships are a major part of our lives. They surround us.

We think about them, talk about them, and experience them. Many we develop thinking they'll be permanent. But often the stability of the relationship begins to crumble. Why?

In many cases, we can blame our negative self-talk. Our toxic thoughts can impact relationships with our spouse, our parents, our siblings, our co-workers, our children, our friends.

Hot Thoughts That Sabotage Your Communication

When relationships are damaged, it's usually due to a breakdown in the communication process, the link that creates a relationship between people.

Communication helps us become who we are. It can be clear—which leads to understanding—or unclear, which leads to confusion.

Communication can be constructive and build a relationship, or it can be destructive, tearing it down.

Criticism is a form of communication that cuts and destroys. It doesn't seek to resolve conflict or draw a spouse closer. It simply provides a way to feel justified and superior. It's a way to release anger.

When you criticize, you find fault. You're saying to the other person, "You're defective in some way, and I don't accept you."

Criticism can be hidden under the camouflage of humor. When confronted about it, a person will avoid the responsibility by saying, "Hey, I was just joking." It reminds me of the passage in Proverbs: "Like a madman shooting deadly, burning arrows is the one who tricks a neighbor and then says, 'I was just joking'" (Prov. 26:18–19 NCV).

Perfectionistic people use fault-finding, calling it "constructive criticism." But that doesn't nourish a relationship, it poisons it. Criticism comes in many shapes and sizes. Zingers are lethal, verbally guided missiles. A critical zinger comes at you with a sharp point and a jagged barb that catches the flesh as it goes in.

Where does destructive talk originate? From destructive thoughts, hot thoughts. As you've seen in earlier chapters, what occurs within the mind is what shapes the words that are expressed.

Another damaging form of communication that creates major problems in a relationship uses the words "always" and "never" in a negative way:

"You never . . ."

"You always . . ."

We call this "all-or-nothing thinking." We also call statements like these "gunpowder thoughts." If they make their way into dialogue, they're sure to incite a defensive response.

When "You never . . ." or "You always . . ." creeps into your thinking, the person on the other side of the relationship has little chance of being seen as having positive qualities. These words are like insecticide that drifts across a field and kills all the crops, rather than just the weeds.

People on the other side of those words often give up. And rightly so. When we begin thinking in those terms, we've condemned the other person, and probably won't give him or her credit, no matter what.

> We call statements like these "gunpowder thoughts."

These words hinder you from even recognizing expectations, and they become a source of discouragement for both of you. And besides, they're not realistic. No one can live up to "always" or "never" all of the time, whether it's in a positive way or a negative one.

If you find yourself responding like this with your self-talk, you're probably expressing it to others too. But you can catch these hot thoughts and derail them.

You might catch yourself thinking: He's always late, She never listens to me, or They always leave a mess and never clean up.

When you find yourself thinking in these generalizations—using "always" or "never"—stop, and in your mind or on paper, identify at least three exceptions to the behavior you've identified as "always." The only place to use the word "always" is "always look for exceptions."

Try substituting specific thoughts, using words that are realistic and accepting, instead. Try replacing the "always" thoughts or words with statements like these: "I would appreciate knowing when you'll be late. It's difficult for me to use my time wisely," or "Please listen to me when I'm uspet. That's the best way to help me cool down."

When we drop absolute generalizations, and focus instead on the one specific situation at hand, we are better able to resolve issues. Instead of assuming the worst or attributing a negative reason for what occurred, we can give the benefit of the doubt. It works wonders to diffuse hot thoughts that might otherwise explode.

Character assassination is another form of hot thoughts that causes problems. When we blame another's personality as the cause of an issue, rather than blaming circumstances, it's a convenient trap.

Allowing our negative self-talk to take over, we might think: She's late because she's basically irresponsible. That's character assassination. Imagine the consequences of that hot thought.

What if we directed our self-talk in the way of placing responsibility outside the relationship, rather than laying blame? Instead of fuming, we could tell ourselves: She could be late because of all the traffic today.

The Bible tells us in 1 Corinthians 13 that this is the right response. Love gives the other person the benefit of the doubt.

More hot thoughts come from fatalistic, exaggerated predictions that blow one situation out of proportion. For instance, if a husband isn't as affectionate as the wife wants him to be, she might use this kind of thinking, telling herself: It will always be this way; He doesn't find me attractive anymore; or He's interested in someone else.

Once those thoughts come to mind, they begin to expand and become set in. The wife takes out her fears on her husband, transforming her hot thoughts into negative behaviors. She begins pushing her husband away. Damage to the relationship escalates, helping bring about what she feared. Identifying three realistic exceptions to her beliefs, putting them in writing, and verbalizing them in private could have brought about a far different result.

Hot thoughts also stem from suspicion or lack of trust. Taking the role of mind reader, we may see a positive behavior not for what it is, but attribute it to a hidden motive. But reacting to such self-talk can bring dangerous consequences.

We also react wrongly to hot thoughts that come from hopeless-helpless thinking. I've heard husbands and wives say, "Nothing can change or improve our relationship," or "He'll always be like this." Now, *that* is a defeatist belief. It keeps them from attempting to make progress, and it causes them to look at the other person through a negative filter. It could even act as a self-fulfilling prophecy. It certainly will keep you stuck.

Let's take this scenario a step further: Do you know the results of nothing-can-change-or-improve-in-our-relationship self-talk? Even if they don't fit you and your situation, they may fit someone you know.

With a belief such as this, you end up with a sense of resignation: "I'll just have to learn to live with this." You feel powerless, and a downward spiral starts. You begin to think less of yourself, and that usually leads to thinking less of your partner. When that happens, your loving and giving behavior toward your spouse dries up.

I remember hearing one husband say, "I'm afraid my learning to live with it was the first step in learning to live without her." That's sad, especially because in the majority of situations, change and growth *are* possible.

When we begin to think like this—that there's no other option but defeat—we can correct ourselves. We can ask ourselves for proof: Where's the evidence this won't change?

We can also ask ourselves: Am I reinforcing and cultivating this situation with my hot thoughts, my negative self-talk?

We can ask ourselves: What would I think and do if this situation didn't occur again or reversed itself? Then begin responding that way. Go against your thinking. Act "as if."

I've talked with some spouses who feel like martyrs. Once people feel that way, revenge surfaces—either hidden or blatant. It's a hideous cycle that destroys marriages. And it often is nurtured by hot thoughts.

More Common Hot Thoughts That Destroy

Many of our hot thoughts come from assumptions. Usually, assumptions are negative. They portray the worst about another person.

In marriage, we make assumptions that lead to unfavorable judgments. A wife may hear her husband humming and think, He's just doing that to irritate me. He knows that bothers me!

Does she really know that? Can we determine with certainty another person's motives?

Often, when our negative self-talk takes control, we "magnify." This is the tendency to enlarge the qualities of another person, usually in a negative way.

Mark wasn't adept when it came to spending and saving money. Once, when some checks bounced, his wife shared some of her thoughts with me.

"He is such a spendthrift. He does this constantly. We won't have enough money for the bills this month. If we're late on the house payment again, they'll foreclose! We're going to lose our house and it's all because of him!"

I think you can imagine the ensuing conversation between the two.

The Problem of Absolutes

We've talked elsewhere about the problem of "should" statements.

Shoulds are absolutes, and often used in an attempt to control the other person. It also suggests the other person "should" have known what you want or need, without you having to tell them. No one has this ability. This hot thought leads both of you into an arena of frustration.[1]

Hot thoughts that turn into marital warfare stem from blame.

Blame points the finger of responsibility at another. When we blame, we remove responsibility from our own shoulders. In their book *Why Can't You Read My Mind?* authors Jeffrey Bernstein and Susan Magee describe it in this way:

The words "if" and "only" are red flags in the Blame Game. You will know that your relationship is suffering from toxic blaming if you or your partner make statements like "It's not my fault. If only you would stop doing this, we'd be okay," or "If she hadn't opened her big mouth . . ." or "If you were a normal person, you would see that you're emotionally closed."

Blame is about denial. Blame is toxic because it causes one partner to feel shamed by the other. We blame our partners because we are seeking an answer to the question "Who did it?" rather than "What can we do about it?" Blame communicates the desire to punish.[2]

When our thoughts wrap themselves about pinning responsibility on another, our focus is not on solving the problem. Once our self-talk is stuck on blame, we often add to the original offense and it's blown out of proportion. It's like a trial where we become the accuser, the judge, and jury.

If there's a tendency to blame in our thinking, how is this related to anger? Often the two go together.

Ask yourself this question: If I couldn't blame _____ for this, what or who else might be responsible for this problem?

When our minds have a critical or toxic bent, we often tend to be hard on ourselves as well, about issues in which we really have no responsibility. The same evaluative questions suggested above can be applied to ourselves as well.

These are just a handful of possible hot thoughts. Consider the results. In *We Can Work It Out*, the authors point out:

Hot thoughts lead to feelings of hopelessness ("He's never going to change"), anger and resentment ("I don't deserve to be treated like this"), and even depression ("All I want to do is stay in bed, watch TV, and eat"). Hot thoughts also lead directly to destructive patterns of relationship talk. If you feel angry and hopeless, you will say things that communicate these feelings. You are likely to criticize your partner, offer negative problem solutions, mind-read your partner's thoughts and feelings, and fail to utilize listening talk. Because these behaviors tend to elicit replies in kind from your partner, you find yourself in the middle of an argument that confirms your worst thoughts. But it's a vicious cycle. Your thoughts lead to actions that increase the chance of conflict, and the inevitable conflict provides energy for more hot thoughts. You will rapidly find yourself trapped in one or more of the now-familiar patterns of escalation and pursuit → withdrawal.[3]

Hot thoughts usually take the reality of a situation out of the realm of being reality. By using language that isn't accurate or precise, we distort our thinking.

> Hot thoughts usually take the reality of a situation out of the realm of being reality.

It's interesting to note how thinking, language, and emotions relate. Language can shape our thinking; thinking can shape our language. And our thinking and language can shape our emotions and behavior.

Even in strong relationships, we often focus on the negatives in an attempt to make the relationship better. We point out what we don't like, and ignore what the other person does that pleases us.

However, by thinking and dwelling on what's wrong in a relationship, it's easy to lose sight of what is *right*. This is a primary reason why admiration is often the first thing to go.

For example, in a marriage, once you allow your spouse's negative qualities to consume your thoughts, you may forget all the attributes you long admired and valued.

Bringing Peace with "Cool Thoughts"

Have you ever used words like *terrible, awful,* or *devastating* to describe a situation? Probably. What if you used words that were less emotionally charged, describing the situation as *inconvenient* or as an *annoyance*. Wouldn't the resulting emotional response be different?

Using "cool thoughts" like these can take the burn out of hot thoughts.

Think of the mercury in a thermometer. That represents the heat of your emotions. The higher the mercury goes, the hotter your emotions. What causes this heat? It's your beliefs and self-talk.

Now visualize changing your words, turning down the heat in your language with cooler words. What do you think happens in the thermometer? The mercury, and the heat in your emotions, falls.

Whenever we use hot thoughts or hot language, we increase negative emotions, such as anger. And we can affect our health. Research proves that carrying or expressing anger can cause cardiovascular problems.[4]

Consider the impact of cool thoughts on a marriage: A spouse could make great strides in improving, or even saving, a relationship simply by reminding himself or herself that the negative issues don't cancel out all the positives that led them to fall in love. Bad times don't wipe out all the good times.

If your marriage is going through a rocky period, it's particularly important to use cool thoughts. Dwell specifically on happy memories you have of your mate. Force yourself to sit and think about the positives. You can look through photo albums from past vacations or reread old love letters. Cool thoughts can promote growth in relationships, just as hot thoughts cause damage.

The bottom line is that you're the architect of your thoughts. You need to decide how to build them.

You have two options: You can look at what your relationship lacks, and focus on disappointments, filling your mind with thoughts of irritation, hurt, and contempt. Or you can do just the opposite. What will you decide?

If you give in to hot thoughts, without countering and evaluating them, the results will be negative. Consider the examples of thinking errors listed below. As you read each one, indicate in the space provided whether you ever have this type of thought. Write an example of your most recent one. Try to remember what you said to the other person that was based on your thoughts.

- Personalizing is thinking that all situations and events revolve around you.

"I looked out of place at the party—they were all her friends!"

A time I've used this type of negative thinking:

_____

_____

What I said, based on my thoughts:

_____

_____

- Magnifying is blowing negative events out of proportion. "This is the worst thing that could have happened to me!" *A time I've used this type of negative thinking:*

_____

_____

What I said, based on my thoughts:

_____

_____

- Minimizing is glossing over positive factors. "Sure, everything went well with the dinner party. But I still have to wonder if everyone *really* had a good time." *A time I've used this type of negative thinking:*

_____

_____

_____

What I said, based on my thoughts:

_____

_____

- Either/or thinking goes to extremes, leaving no room for realistic options.

"Either I'm a successful spouse or a total failure."

A time I've used this type of negative thinking:

_____

_____

_____

What I said, based on my thoughts:

_____

_____

- Taking events out of context focuses on negatives, despite the presence of positives.

"That comment he made at lunch ruined the whole day."

A time I've used this type of negative thinking:

_____

_____

_____

What I said, based on my thoughts:

_____

_____

_____

- Jumping to conclusions runs ahead of rational thinking.

"My spouse isn't paying me as much attention. Her love for me is fading."

A time I've used this type of negative thinking:

_____

_____

What I said, based on my thoughts:

_____

_____

- Overgeneralizing uses thinking based on "always" or "never."

"I never can please him. I constantly blow it as a married partner," or "He never does anything for me. And he'll always be this way."

A time I've used this type of negative thinking:

_____

_____

_____

What I said, based on my thoughts:

_____

_____

_____

- Self-blame condemns the total person, rather than specific behaviors that can be changed.

"I'm no good as a parent."

A time I've used this type of negative thinking:

_____

_____

_____

What I said, based on my thoughts:

_____

_____

_____

- Mind reading assumes you know someone else's thoughts.

"She thinks I'm a loser."

A time I've used this type of negative thinking:

_____

_____

_____

What I said, based on my thoughts:

_____

_____

- Comparing creates an unfair assessment that often ignores basic difference.

"He's just much smarter than I am."

A time I've used this type of negative thinking:

What I said, based on my thoughts:

Consider ways to counter these toxic thinking patterns. For example, a wife overgeneralizes, telling herself: I'll never be able to satisfy my husband. I've made too many mistakes these first three years of marriage.

Imagine the difference in her behavior if she countered that erroneous thinking with cooler self-talk like this: I don't know that I won't be able to satisfy him. I can grow and develop as a person. I can change. Where's the evidence that I'll *never* be able to? Here is what I will attempt today . . .

Imagine the impact of these thoughts on someone who minimizes in his thinking, disqualifying everything positive. Example: My work isn't exciting or challenging at all. My life isn't fulfilling anymore.

What if he turned those hot thoughts around with cooler thinking, such as: My work may not be exciting, but there is a purpose to it. My work helps other people. And just because my work isn't thrilling, who says the rest of my life can't be great? There are lots of things I can do to enrich my life.

A wife may react with negative behavior toward her husband, just because she had hot thoughts based on jumping to conclusions. She fumes, I'll probably mess up this recipe his mom used to make. Then he'll be annoyed, and will probably ignore me for the rest of the evening.

She could halt that downward spiral before hot thoughts ruin the evening, by challenging them like this: I don't have to be a perfect cook. I can make it better the next time, if it doesn't turn out well. If he's disappointed, I can let him know that I'm disappointed too, but it's not the end of the world.

Mind reading gets in the way of relationships when we think things like, What's the point in doing that for her? She wouldn't like it, or might not even notice.

Instead, we can think: I have no way of knowing. I can at least try. I need to give her a chance to respond. I might be surprised. If she doesn't care, it's not the end of the world.[5]

Let me make one last suggestion. Think about this: What if, for the rest of the day, you committed to God every thought you have about other people? This passage of Scripture could be your guide as you think about others:

"Therefore, as God's chosen people, holy and dearly loved, clothe yourselves with compassion, kindness, humility, gentleness and patience. Bear with each other and forgive whatever grievances you may have against one another. Forgive as the Lord forgave you" (Col. 3:12–13 NIV).

Purposely make every thought about the people around you positive and reflective of the words you just read. If you begin a negative thought, correct it. This is the time to apply everything you've learned so far. It can and will make a difference.

Reflect and Remember

1. What did you learn about hot thoughts and your thought life?

   _____

   _____

   _____

2. Keep track of how many times you use the words *always* or *never*. What could you substitute for these words?

   _____

   _____

   _____

3. What can you do to give others the benefit of the doubt?

   _____

   _____

   _____

4. Which of the following best characterizes the negative thinking you do most?

> character assassination
>
> suspicion or lack of trust
>
> negative predictions
>
> hopeless or helpless thinking
>
> assuming
>
> overgeneralization
>
> blame

Emotions and Your Thoughts

Gary sat in his car, where he'd been for the last twenty minutes . . . stuck in gridlock on the expressway. In the next lane over, Tony sat too.

Both were going to be late for an appointment. Both were immobilized by traffic. What was different was their response.

Tony looked around, enjoying the scenery, while he played calming music.

Gary wasn't just angry—he was fuming. His mind was alive with what he thought about other stupid drivers; the highway workers; his boss, for scheduling a meeting at the worst possible time of day.

Gary and Tony—two men stuck in a situation beyond their control. One calm, one angry. One accepted the delay; one fought it.

Tony could have been just as upset, just as angry. He chose a different path in his thoughts than Gary, and experienced very different results.

In his book *Highway to Dynamic Living*, Loren Fischer writes: "The steam of behavior is only visible proof that the fire of thought is boiling the water of emotion. A heavy lid may curb the steam of action but unless we curb the fire of thinking the heaviest lid possible will blow and high will be the blast of it. Obviously, therefore, we lose spiritual battles not by failing to restrain our actions with heavier lids, we are defeated because we do not change our flaming thoughts that boil the waters of emotion."[1]

We were created as emotional beings. And our emotions affect us in countless ways.

Have you ever tried to fall asleep when you were upset? Instead of drifting peacefully off to sleep, your mind raced 101 mph as you tossed and turned.

Have you ever waited outside an office for an interview, with your heart pounding wildly, perspiration on your brow, and your mouth bone-dry? Have you ever become so upset or angry with another person that you couldn't think what to say?

Emotions may arise from external circumstances, or they may be triggered from within . . . by our thoughts.

Emotions can be experienced as both pleasant and painful. We automatically associate pleasant feelings with positive emotions, and painful feelings with negative. Feelings also can be a signal of impending danger, or a warning that something is wrong.

But emotions have gotten a bad name with some of us because they can be unreliable, inconsistent, and difficult to understand. They don't always make sense.

In themselves, emotions aren't good or bad, right or wrong, healthy or unhealthy—they simply *are*. It's the way we learn to deal with our emotions that causes us problems.

Emotional maturity involves deciding how we choose to express the feelings we experience. The best place to start in looking at our emotions is where the Bible starts—with Creation. In Genesis 1:26–27, we see: "Then God said, 'Let us make man in our image, in our likeness, and let them rule over the fish of the sea and the birds of the air, over the livestock, over all the earth, and over all the creatures that move along the ground.' So God created man in his own image, in the image of God he created him; male and female he created them" (NIV).

> Emotional maturity involves deciding how we choose to express the feelings we experience.

When God made us in his image, he gave us a mind, a will, and emotions. The mind gives us the ability to think. Our emotions provide the ability to feel. Our will allows us the opportunity to choose.

God intentionally designed those three parts—the mind, emotions, and will—to work together in balance and harmony, like the legs of a three-legged milking stool. Each dimension of our personality is important and necessary.

Dorothy Finkelhor, in *How to Make Your Emotions Work for You*, says that emotions are:

the motivating forces of our lives, driving us to go ahead, pushing us backward, stopping us completely, determining what we do, how we feel, what we want, and whether we get what we want. Our hates, loves, fears, and what to do about them are determined by our emotional structure. There is nothing in our lives that does not have the emotional factor as its mainspring. It gives us power, or makes us weak, operates for our benefit or to our detriment, for our happiness or confusion.[2]

In *Renovation of the Heart*, Dallas Willard explains:

Feelings are a primary blessing *and* a primary problem for human life. We cannot live without them and we can hardly live with them. . . . In the restoration of the individual to God, feelings too must be renovated: old ones removed in many cases, or at least thoroughly modified, and new ones installed or at least heightened into a new prominence.

Our first inquiry as we greet people for the day is likely to be, "How are you feeling today?" Rarely will it be, "How are you thinking?" Feelings live on the front row of our lives like unruly children clamoring for attention. They presume on their justification in being whatever they are—unlike a thought, which by nature is open to challenge and invites the question "Why?"

The term "feeling" indicates a kind of "contact," a "touch," that is at once blind and powerful—in allure as well as in revulsion. A "touching" scene is one that evokes feelings, that "touches" us. In feelings we really know that something is "there," and solidly so.[3]

Feelings move us and we enjoy this. They give us a sense of being alive. Without them, we have little interest in things. When people say they've "lost interest in life," it means their feelings are flat. Some turn to substances or activities that help them feel alive. The Scriptures describe times that Jesus was moved by the feeling of compassion.

Our emotions are no accident. Sometimes our emotions are a warning sign that something else is occurring in our lives. Sometimes God speaks to us through our emotions. Some of us live more with our thoughts; and some more in their emotions. In his book *Real Men Have Feelings Too*, Dr. Gary Oliver writes: "God has designed us in such a way that our emotions influence almost every aspect of our lives. God speaks to us through our emotions. They are like a sixth sense. Emotions are to our personality what gasoline is to a car. They are the source of our passion and intensity. They help us to monitor our needs, make us aware of good and evil, provide motivation and energy."[4]

The fruit of the Spirit, described in Galatians 5:22–23, is based on emotions—love, joy, peace, patience, and gentleness. David spoke of emotion when he wrote, "I am fearfully and wonderfully made" (Ps. 139:14 NIV).

Nowhere is the delicate complexity of God's creation more evident than in our emotional makeup. Emotions are complex. We frequently feel loved, happy, anxious, fearful, hurt, frustrated, embarrassed, humiliated, angry, depressed, excited, sad, scared, lonely, or proud.

Our thoughts are tied to these emotions. You can build and create your love for another by your thoughts, just as you can kill your love for another by what you think.

Emotional Bad Habits

When you find yourself upset emotionally, look for the link to your thoughts. It's like using the internet. We have to click on the link to find what we're seeking. When you think about what you were thinking before you became upset, you'll probably find the link between your thoughts and emotions.

Negative self-talk develops negative emotional habits. It's a response you learn, and it becomes automatic because you use it so much. It's like an addiction, only a negative thinking pattern is the drug of choice.

Negative emotions, created by negative thoughts, are habits, just like your self-talk is a habit. They're not necessarily tied to your personality. It's not a matter of genes. And because of that, there's hope for change. What's been learned can be unlearned.

In *When Am I Going to Be Happy?* Penelope Russvanoff points out:

> Emotional bad habits are losing games like playing against an opponent with loaded dice. As long as you keep playing with them, you will keep on losing.
>
> Strange—while negative emotions stick to us like tar, our positive, healthy, happy feelings are often fleeting and fragile. Good moods are shattered by the mildest reversals and instantly replaced by bad moods. A law of emotions seems to be at work here. Bad feelings drive out good feelings. The habit of looking at things negatively is so ingrained in some that they dismiss even past happy experiences as no longer valid. They create "retroactive misery."[5]

Let's get back to the brain: We won't be able to really change our thoughts unless we understand how much our brain is involved. The changes we want to make involve changes in the brain. And this can happen.

Within the brain there is a section of memory banks. When a thought is created within the brain or enters it, a section of the brain called the thalamus goes to work. The thalamus makes sense of the thought, and runs it through the memory banks. There it's assessed by another portion of the brain, the amygdala. That's the storehouse of memories.

When your thoughts are toxic or negative, you've handed off control to your emotions, which are not always reliable. Their chemical nature gives them this control. The amygdala has its place and its purpose, part of which is to alert us. But unless it's brought into balance by nontoxic balanced thoughts, the emotions it generates dominate.[6]

The Link between Our Thoughts and Our Anger

Scripture gives numerous examples of angry individuals: "Then Saul became very angry with Jonathan. He said, 'You son of a wicked, worthless woman! I know you are on the side of David.' . . . Then Saul threw his spear at Jonathan, trying to kill him" (1 Sam. 20:30, 33 NCV).

Saul didn't think first. In fact, he didn't think at all.

Another man in the Bible became angry, and was actually justified in his anger. A number of poor, homeless people were taken advantage of by princes and rulers. They took what little the poor had. It wasn't fair, so they complained to Nehemiah. Here is what he did: "When I heard their outcry and these charges, I was very angry. I pondered them in my mind and then accused the nobles and officials. I told them,

'You are exacting usury from your own countrymen!' So I called together a large meeting to deal with them" (Neh. 5:6–7 NIV).

Notice the wording here. He thought it over. The NASB translation says, "I consulted with myself." Nehemiah became calm and rational by using his self-talk.

Let's consider anger in your life.

How frequently do you experience anger?

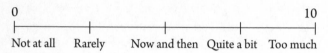

What would you say are the major causes for anger in your life?

1. _____

2. _____

3. _____

It's so easy to put the responsibility for our anger onto others.

"She made me angry."

"If he hadn't done that . . ."

"If that supervisor would treat us better . . ."

Self-talk often causes our emotional response. And when our self-talk contains the word *must*, it's a demand—a demand that will cause anger when it isn't met.

I must . . .

He must . . .

They must . . .

Sometimes, if the demand isn't met, we pile on more negative self-talk, such as, "I can't tolerate that!"

As we've seen before, our thinking is full of errors. And sometimes our thoughts are contrary to Scripture.

It's harsh, but true. Often our thoughts are self-centered, rather than centered on others. It becomes a vicious cycle when our anger is fueled by this rehearsal of negative self-talk.

Many are raised to believe it's their right not only to get angry but to stay angry. When this happens, anger continues. I've heard many say:

"But . . . you don't know what I'm dealing with."

"It's so frustrating what those idiots are doing."

"They shouldn't treat me that way."

"What they're doing is wrong. They shouldn't get away with that."

"Why should I have to take that?"

Are you aware of your angry thoughts? Often we don't want to admit that our self-talk is angry. But so often, that's where anger and angry behavior start.

Just before leaving for his Saturday morning golf game, Art asked his eleven-year-old son to clean up his room and wash the family car. Jimmy said he would.

When Art returned home, Jimmy was nowhere to be seen. His room was only half clean, and the car was still a mess. Listen in on Art's inner conversation as he surveys the scene:

"Where is that boy? He didn't follow my instructions. He's so lazy and inconsiderate. I give him everything, and he doesn't even have the courtesy to do a little work. He never follows through. Wait till I see him. And he always leaves without writing a note telling me where he's going. I'll ground that kid for a month!"

You may argue that Art had the right to be frustrated and angry. Maybe so. Maybe not.

Regardless, Art was free to choose how he thought about the scene before him. His inner conversation reveals that he chose to fuel his frustration with distorted thinking. He resorted to labeling, calling Jimmy lazy and inconsiderate. Labeling encourages frustration because it perpetuates a negative view. When you allow yourself to label, you begin to look for behaviors that reinforce the labels you've attached to other people. You tend to overlook the positives and look for the worst.

Another evidence of Art's distorted thinking is magnification. Words like *never* and *always* magnify occasional misbehaviors, painting them as lifetime habits. Magnifying others' misbehavior only serves to intensify frustration.

Art's inner conversation was based on hasty, negative assumptions. Perhaps an emergency in the neighborhood called Jimmy from his task. It could have been that an out-of-town relative arrived unexpectedly and took Jimmy to the mall for the afternoon. Perhaps a shut-in down the street called Jimmy to run an important errand. Maybe he left a note explaining his whereabouts. Art was so busy thinking the worst, he didn't look for it.

You'll save yourself a lot of frustration and anger if you learn to base your inner conversations on hard facts and positive assumptions.

So how can you better become aware of your self-talk, especially when anger is present? Someone suggested training the ear of your imagination to listen to what you're saying to yourself—close your eyes and ignore all sounds around you. Turn off *all* electronics, and concentrate on the talk that's occurring in your mind. The more you allow yourself to concentrate on it, the more you'll hear. In time you won't have to close your eyes.

> **Train the ear of your imagination to listen to what you're saying to yourself.**

We don't like to admit that we're angry, and that *we're* responsible for it. My friend Dr. Gary Oliver has written extensively on this subject. In his book *Real Men Have Feelings Too*, he said: "Acknowledging our anger sounds simple, but for many it's easier said than done. Due to its negative reputation and people's tendency to deny it, anger has been called the 'most likely to be mislabeled' emotion."[7]

Recognizing that we experience anger can be difficult. I encourage you to make a copy of the word list below. Then for a two-week period, put a check mark by each word that describes what you're experiencing. You may find you have checked some words many times:

Aggravated	Furious	Offended	Slow burn
Annoyed	Grumpy	Out of sorts	Stew
Aroused	Hot	Provoked	Temper
Bitter	Huffy	Rant	Touchy
Burned up	Ill-tempered	Rave	Vexed
Cranky	Indignant	Repulsed	Vicious
Cross	Irritated	Riled	Worked up
Exasperated	Miffed	Sarcastic	Wounded

You probably find it difficult to say the "A" word (*anger*). But be comforted in this: You have a lot of company.

One of the most effective ways to work through this barrier is to start by silently acknowledging your anger to yourself. Then, when you are alone and are aware of being angry, say the "A" word: Say to yourself aloud, "I think I may be angry." If you have no doubts about it, simply say, "I'm angry!" Feel free to let your volume and tone of voice accurately reflect the intensity of your anger.

Next, find a confidante, and tell him or her about your anger. You'll find that the simple act of acknowledging and talking about your anger with someone will decrease your discomfort and fear.

It rarely helps to "try hard" to stop being angry. What does help is to acknowledge that you are angry, identify the root causes—usually from self-talk—and redirect the energy away from attacking a person, to attacking the problem.

Once you have acknowledged you're angry, before doing anything else, take it to the Lord in prayer. He created us and has given us his Spirit. Through prayer, he can help us with the cause and the solution.

The Emotions behind Our Anger

Often our self-talk clusters around the three main underlying causes of anger—fear, hurt, or frustration.

If you're experiencing fear, ask yourself, What am I saying to myself about my fear? How am I turning this into anger?

If you're experiencing hurt, ask yourself, What am I saying to myself about my hurt? How am I turning this into anger?

If you're experiencing frustration, ask yourself, What am I saying to myself about my frustration? How am I turning this into anger?

People have said to me again and again statements like this: "Norm, I don't want to talk in an angry way to others, especially my family, but something just comes over me and I let it rip! There's a limit to what I can take. I know I really love them, but sometimes I don't like them very much. I don't know what to do to change."

I usually respond with a question: "When you feel frustrated and angry with your family members, what do you focus on? How they react at what you said, or how you would like them to act?"

They usually respond with something like, "Oh, I keep mulling over what I didn't like, as well as my destructive comments. I relive it again and again and beat up on myself for hurting them."

> When you spend so much time thinking about what you shouldn't have done, you reinforce the negative behavior.

I ask: "Do you realize that by rehearsing your failures, you're programming yourself to repeat them?"

They respond with a puzzled look. But it's true. When you spend so much time thinking about what you shouldn't have done, you reinforce the negative behavior.

Furthermore, spending all your time and energy mentally rehashing your failures keeps you from formulating what you really *want* to do. Redirecting your time and energy toward a solution will make a big difference in how you communicate. Focus your attention on how you want to respond to your frustration, and you *will* experience change!

If you know you're going to be in a situation that could activate your self-talk and anger, choose some preventative self-talk. Perhaps it's a person who's difficult. Maybe it's a frustration at work, or a difficult family get-together, or traffic. Here are some examples of preventative self-talk:

No matter what he says or does, I can handle it. I've asked God to give me grace.

I don't know what kind of day they've had if they're irritable. I can ask them about it and then pray quietly.

With God's help I will be able to stay calm and I will slow down my rate of talking.

If I start to get angry, I'll take some deep breaths and slow down my rate of talking.

I give him permission not to be agreeable or to be out of sorts. I can handle it.

It's all right to be stuck in traffic. It's not the end of the world. I can call ahead and then use the time to pray and go over Scripture.

If you suddenly find yourself in a situation you didn't anticipate, and you begin to get angry, you can "debrief" yourself. Debriefing is a technique used with those who've been in a traumatic experience such as an accident, shooting, or disaster. It involves describing what has been experienced, and the thoughts and feelings that went along with that. The purpose of debriefing is to help in coping.

Here are some self-debriefing statements you can repeat in your mind:

I don't have to be angry over this. Why should I let them control my emotions?

I'll feel so much better about myself not getting angry.

This is so great not getting upset. This really works.

I can take this energy and get angry, or pray for him.

I know this isn't what I want, but neither is anger.

It's okay to be stuck in traffic and late for the meeting. I can handle it.

I'm going to follow this Scripture: "He who is slow to anger is better than the mighty, he who rules his [own] spirit than he who takes a city" (Prov. 16:32 AMP).

I'm going to remember: "Good sense makes a man restrain his anger, and it is his glory to overlook a transgression or an offense" (Prov. 19:11 AMP).

It's all right for this to not work out the way I wanted. I can adjust.

I can learn from this experience, and use it to glorify God.

I'm God's creation and not man's. I want to reflect him.

Self-talk will reinforce your efforts to diffuse anger in the future. Tell yourself, using positive self-talk, that you did well. Thank God for your growth and then tell yourself what you'll do next time.[8]

Remember that when you rehearse your anger over and over again, you feed it and keep it alive. When you let it go, it fades away.

In *Prescription for Anger*, authors Gary and Carol Hankins suggest this exercise to diminish anger:

Make a tight fist. (If you have long fingernails, make your grip such that your fingernails aren't digging into your hand.) Keep your fist tight while you count out sixty seconds. Once you reach forty, intensify your squeeze with each count. Even though your hand aches and the pain keeps getting stronger, hold your fist tighter and tighter until you finish the count to sixty. The physical pain you feel represents the mental and emotional pain that accompanies your anger. Now *slowly* begin to relax your grip. Take about fifteen seconds to open your hand, then let it return to a relaxed position in your lap. As you gently let go of your tight grip, notice the pleasant sensation of the tenseness and pain melting away. You are freeing your hand of its discomfort, enabling it to return to its maximum usefulness. Similarly, when you let go of your anger you free yourself of mental and emotional pain and enable yourself to experience life to its fullest.[9]

Use your self-talk to let go. Tell yourself aloud, "I'm letting go of my anger. I don't need to hold on to this anger."

There is one other step to relinquish your anger, especially if you've been wronged. It's called forgiveness.

When we fail to forgive, we inflict inner torment upon ourselves.

When we forgive, we feel a burden lifted. We say: It's all right; it's over. I no longer resent you or see you as an enemy. I love you even if you cannot love me back.

Dr. Sidney Simon and Suzanne Simon say,

> Forgiveness is letting go of the intense emotions attached to incidents from our past. We still remember what happened, but we no longer feel intensely angry, frightened, bitter, resentful, or damaged because of it. . . .
>
> Forgiveness is recognizing that we no longer *need* our grudges and resentments, our hatred and self-pity. We do not need them as an excuse for getting less out of life than we want or deserve. . . .
>
> Forgiveness is no longer wanting to punish the people who hurt us. It is no longer wanting to get even or to have them suffer as much as we did. . . .
>
> . . . Forgiveness is freeing up and putting to better use the energy once consumed by holding grudges, harboring resentments, and nursing unhealed wounds. [Anger needs the experience of forgiveness to bring it to a close.] Forgiveness is moving on.[10]

There is one other step to relinquishing anger. You might need to forgive yourself. Why? There are several reasons. You might be blaming yourself and feeling guilty for:

- Not being able to change your self-talk quickly enough
- Not living up to others' expectations for you
- Not being loved and accepted by others
- Not being perfect

- Treating yourself the way others treated you
- Mistreating yourself when you have difficult times as a result of your past
- Developing some of the same tendencies or problems you despise in others

Isn't it ironic that we often take out our frustrations on ourselves? We can choose to focus on ourselves as victims. Or we can see ourselves as people who can overcome difficulties through God's grace and his guidance in changing our thoughts.

There is a reason why God inspired men to write the Scriptures and why he preserved his words through the centuries for us: They are supreme guidelines for life. Regardless of what you may have experienced or been taught in the past, God's plan works! In a journal, write out each of the following verses from Proverbs (quoted here in NIV):

> Reckless words pierce like a sword,
>> but the tongue of the wise brings healing.
>> (12:18)

> A patient man has great understanding,
>> but a quick-tempered man displays folly.
>> (14:29)

> Better a patient man than a warrior,
>> a man who controls his temper than one who takes a city. (16:32)

Add other Scriptures you discover that relate to frustration and anger. Read these verses aloud morning and evening for three weeks, and you'll own them.

You'll be able to change your angry thinking only if you plan to change. Your intentions may be good, but once the frustration-anger sequence kicks into gear, your ability to think clearly is limited.

Identify in advance what you want to say when you begin to feel frustrated or angry with people. Be specific. Write out your responses and read them aloud to yourself, and maybe even to a trusted friend.

In my counseling office, I often have clients practice their new responses on me, and I attempt to respond as the other person might. By practicing on me, they are able to refine their statements, eliminate their anxiety or feelings of discomfort, and gain confidence for their new approach.

Reflect and Remember

1. When you hear the word *emotions*, what comes to mind?

_____

_____

_____

2. What decisions have you made based on your emotions? What were the thoughts that created those emotions?

_____

_____

_____

_____

3. How have emotions enhanced your life?

4. What could you do to "consult with yourself" when you're angry?

5. What will you do now to become more aware of your self-talk and the relationship to anger?

6. Which Scriptures would help you deal with anger in a positive way?

Your Thoughts, Worry, and Depression

Kathy struggled to get out of bed in the morning. She could hardly get her head off the pillow. There was a veil of darkness in her mind, and everything looked gloomy. The thought of tackling everyday tasks overwhelmed her. The cause: depression.

Kathy felt as though a committee had taken over her mind, and one member after another was throwing a depressive thought at her. Each one felt like a punishment—they were all so condemning and negative. Everything positive disappeared.

Kathy wished her mind wasn't so active. She wanted it to go blank. But instead, her thoughts were beating her to death. She was seeing her world through dark-tinted glasses. She believed the untrue statements about herself. Her depression deepened.

Anxiety and worry—they seem to be constant companions in our life. When you hear the word *anxiety*, what comes to mind? Being on edge, jumpy, hyperalert, or vigilant?

Anxiety actually has a number of faces. It could be a sense of tension or nervousness just before a final exam or annual review. It could be butterflies (or vultures) in your stomach before a critical presentation. It could be a racing heart as you ask someone special for a date, or as your car slides on ice in a snowstorm. Anxiety has a positive side. It alerts you, and puts you on guard. A little is all right.

Too much disrupts your life. Three decades ago, I experienced a trauma by witnessing a train wreck. I could actually see the car and train converging in my mind seconds before it happened, and I sat there yelling at the train to stop, before it plowed into the small car attempting to sneak around the crossing bars. The Volkswagen was destroyed. Miraculously, the driver survived.

I can still picture this event clearly. And as I drove over those tracks twice a day, five days a week on my way to and from the university, I was affected by anxiety.

For years following the accident, when I was still about a hundred yards from the crossing, my body would tense. Even though I wasn't consciously remembering the incident, I became overly alert and on guard. I'd find myself slowing down and almost coming to a halt, just before crossing the tracks. Other drivers probably wondered, "What's his problem?"

I didn't intend to become hypervigilant, but my brain had other ideas. And the brain controls the body.

Were you aware that your brain cells actually talk to one another? They do. Dr. Archibald Hart gives an insightful description of this process:

> Knowing how brain cells "talk" to each other is crucial to your understanding of anxiety. The reason so many people feel helpless in the face of emotional turmoil is that they don't know enough about what is going on in their brains; to them, the process seems too mysterious, too enigmatic.
>
> But it's not all that complicated. You will feel more in control of your destiny if you know what is going on in your brain.
>
> Conversations are going on between your brain cells all the time. The vital group of chemicals called "neuro-transmitters" are the messengers, and their language consists of minute reactions that "fire" nerve cells. Neuro-transmitters carry messages between different parts of the brain. Not only do they transport information, but they spur some nerve cells to be more activated and responsive while calming and forcing others to slow down and remain quiet.
>
> These chemical messengers pick up, transport, and then deposit their instructions all over the brain, like the pony-express riders of early western times.
>
> Pony-express riders are a good analogy for the messengers that travel through our brain. Nerves are their pathways, and synapses are the pony-express stations that refresh them. Messages carried by neurotransmitters are often life-giving. They tell different parts of the brain whether to be happy or sad, anxious or tranquil. They help the brain decide whether there is a state of emergency or

a danger to be avoided. Likewise, they also tell the brain when to relax because all is safe.

On a typical day in the life of your brain, literally trillions of messages are sent and received by these neurotransmitters.[1]

The authors of *Seeing in the Dark* describe the process in this way:

Have you ever heard of the telephone game? To play this game, participants line up so that each can whisper to their immediate neighbor without being overheard by anyone else. The person at the beginning of the line thinks of a phrase and whispers it to the next person. The message is passed down the line, whisper by whisper, until it reaches the last person. Each person listening hears it a little differently, so by the time it comes out the other end of the "telephone line," the sentence or phrase becomes hilariously garbled!

Your brain is like the telephone game, only a *lot* more complicated. *Millions* of nerve cells line up along predetermined routes to "whisper" messages to one another. They also branch off in many directions to define a network we don't fully understand. Thoughts, emotions, sensations, movement, and countless other activities emerge from this wonderful labyrinth of human flesh and electrical impulses. Under the microscope, the "wiring" in your brain looks like a tangled, chaotic mess. Yet your brain is meticulously and miraculously organized to accomplish all the activities of life. There is a "method to the madness." We *are* fearfully and wonderfully made, but because we live in a fallen and imperfect world, things can go wrong.[2]

Other things can affect the brain too, like illnesses, substance abuse, and injury.

When it comes to anxiety and worry, toxic thinking also plays a major part. Stress is often the result of what we say to ourselves.

Worry is a misuse of thoughts. When we worry, we allow our thinking to spin out of control. Where it starts out and where it ends up can be miles apart, all because of runaway thinking.

A person who doesn't allow thoughts to run wild may realize: I might be late for work today. He or she may then think, I might be or I might not. If so, I can put in some time during lunch. It's not the end of the world.

But a worrier takes a different path and allows toxic thinking to dominate:

If I'm late for my meeting, everyone will notice and wonder. When my supervisor sees I'm late, she'll wonder about my commitment to the company and note this in my file for my next review. My next review won't go well, and I'll miss out on my bonus. Without the bonus we can't get the second car we need. If we can't get that car, Jim won't be able to work after school, and won't be able to save money for college. If he can't get to college, he won't get the education he needs for his future career. If I can't help my son with college, I'll feel like I failed him and I feel worthless.

> When it comes to anxiety and worry, toxic thinking also plays a major part.

Imagine how the person feels at this point all because of worry running rampant.[3]

Has this pattern of thinking ever occurred in your life? You see how easy it is to take one thought, run with it, and end up consumed by negative thoughts?

Worry, Anxiety, and Scripture

Let's consider what Scripture says about anxiety. We see in John 14:1, Jesus said, "Let not your heart be troubled" (KJV).

Is he saying anxiety—all anxiety—is wrong? I don't think so.

There are different forms of anxiety, and in the Bible, one word is used for all of them. It seems that Scripture focuses on the form of anxiety that we call worry. We also call it fretting.

Psalm 37:1 (AMP) begins, "Fret not," and those words are repeated later in the psalm. The dictionary defines *fret* as "to eat away, gnaw, gall, vex, worry, agitate, wear away."

I'm reminded of the scene I see each year when I hike along the Snake River in Grand Teton National Park in Wyoming. Colonies of beavers live along the riverbanks, and often I see trees at various stages of being gnawed to the ground by them. Some trees have slight rings around their trunks where the beavers have just started to chew on them. Other trees have several inches of bark eaten away, and some have already fallen to the ground because the beavers have gnawed through the trunks. Worry has the same effect on us: It will gradually eat away at us until it destroys us.

Worry plagues many of us. The going over and over an issue again and again in our mind is toxic. It's not productive. And when worry takes hold of our thought life, we have a problem.

Worry is not just thinking about things. It becomes worry when those thoughts take on a life of their own. In *The Anxiety Cure*, Dr. Hart says that worry has been described as "a chain of negative and relatively uncontrollable thoughts and images," and as "interest paid in advance on a debt you may never owe."[4]

Worry self-talk overflows with emotion. It tends to reach out for additional emotional connections. Our imagination expands our worry. It exaggerates the problem and blows it out of proportion. Reality is usually ignored.

When we worry it's as though our thoughts get stuck on a circular path and keep coming back to the original thought. But each time we revisit it, there's more emotion and intensity. Our thoughts revolve endlessly, but there's no solution. We keep energizing the worrisome thought.

Sometimes we may not be aware of the repetitious thoughts. But they're still there, like a leaden weight, a heaviness on our heart and mind. That's residue from the constant self-talk about the worry.

Remember your brain is involved. When you worry excessively, your brain is heavily impacted. The more you worry about something (hours a day, week after week) it's as though one of your brain's "switching stations" gets stuck.

Think of it like a cramp in a leg muscle. It stays, regardless of what you do.

Over time, our worrying can cause a brain cramp. It won't let go.

The more we worry, the more a groove is cut into the brain, leading to that worry. The worry finds a home in which to reside. That's why suggestions like, "Don't worry" or "Just relax" don't work.

Jesus had something to say to us about this. It was brief. "Therefore do not worry about tomorrow, for tomorrow will worry about itself. Each day has enough trouble of its own" (Matt. 6:34 NIV).

Jesus gave a simple, direct statement. Don't do it. Don't use your mind to focus on the future—focus on today. I like the description James R. Beck and David T. Moore give in *Helping Worriers*:

> We think there are several reasons why Jesus said what he did about worry. First of all, worry accuses God of being a liar. God has promised to meet all your needs (Phil. 4:19). Needs are one of the things we worry about. Worry blatantly disagrees and argues that God is either unable or unwilling to fulfill that promise in your life. Second, worry questions the sovereignty of God. He has promised to use everything that comes into our lives for good (Rom. 8:28). God is never caught by surprise. Worry finds a thousand reasons why God's promise cannot possibly be true under the current circumstances. Further, worry questions the sincerity of God. God has promised that he will never abandon you. In Hebrews 13:5–6 God states: "Never will I leave you; never will I forsake you." Worry erodes away our faith, and causes us to wonder if God will really be there when we need him. Apparently, the confidence of God's presence was enough for the writer of Hebrews, since he went on to say, "So we say with confidence, 'The Lord is my helper; I will not be afraid. What can man do to me?'"

Worry denies and ignores all of these promises. It plays the "yeah-but" game: "Yeah but, what if the doctor finds something wrong?" "Yeah but, you don't know my husband." "Yeah but, there are times when the Lord has not come through for me the way he should." The "yeah-buts" of life are endless. The problem is, worry knows them all and enjoys playing the game. The "yeah-buts" of worry force your eyes off God and onto something that might or might not happen. Suddenly, you are living in the world of fantasy and fear. Whether your fears become reality or not is irrelevant to the game. Once the focus is off of God, your potential problems (underscore the word "potential") will loom larger than life.[5]

Putting Worry to Rest . . . for Good!

Psychiatrist Edward Hallowell has developed an approach called EPR to combat worry.[6] It stands for Evaluate, Plan, and Remediate.

It's an approach that turns worry into action. It's a form of plan-making. And if we make it a habit, it can defeat the negative impact of worry. Here is an example:

Perhaps you've had some shooting pains in your lower back that come and go. One day they're there, the next day they're not. But the pattern has persisted for several weeks. You read a couple of articles that appear to describe the same symptoms that you're having—but the outcome for the individual described was terminal cancer. After reading this, your mind takes over, because the seeds of worry were planted. Now the worry intensifies. Self-talk and toxic thinking take over.

To use EPR, you could follow these steps:

Evaluate: Make this your new self-talk: This is a new condition for me. The pain is not overwhelming, but annoying. I don't like the pattern it's developing. It doesn't seem to be going away on its own.

Plan: I don't know the causes or what this means. I know I avoid doctors, but the persistence of this means I need to talk to a doctor.

Remediate: You call your doctor and make an appointment.

Here's another method that can break the pattern of worry. A number of years ago I was teaching on the subject of worry. I asked the class to report on an experience I'd suggested the previous week for eliminating worry from their lives. One woman said she began the experiment Monday morning, and by Friday she felt the worry pattern that had plagued her for years was finally broken.

What accomplished this radical improvement? It was a simple method of applying God's Word to her life in a new way.

Take a blank index card and on one side write the word *STOP* in large, bold letters. On the other side type up the complete text of Philippians 4:6–9 (I especially like the Amplified Bible translation):

> Do not fret or have any anxiety about anything, but in every circumstance and in everything, by prayer and petition [definite requests], with thanksgiving, continue to make your wants known to God. And God's peace [shall be yours, that tranquil state of a soul assured of its salvation through Christ, and so fearing nothing from God and content with its earthly lot whatever sort that is, that peace] which transcends all understanding shall garrison and mount guard over your hearts and minds in Christ Jesus. For the rest, brethren, whatever is true, whatever is worthy of reverence and is honorable and seemly, whatever is just, whatever is pure, whatever is lovely and lovable, whatever is kind and

winsome and gracious, if there is any virtue and excellence, if there is anything worthy of praise, think on and weigh and take account of these things [fix your minds on them]. Practice what you have learned and received and heard and seen in me, and model your way of living on it, and the God of peace (of untroubled, undisturbed well-being) will be with you.

It's interesting to note that God says he will guard our hearts, but we are to guard our minds. Keep the card with you at all times. Whenever you're alone and begin to worry, take the card out, hold the STOP side in front of you, and say aloud, "Stop!" twice with emphasis. Then turn the card over and read the Scripture passage aloud twice with emphasis.

> It's interesting to note that God says he will guard our hearts, but we are to guard our minds.

Taking the card out interrupts your thought pattern of worry. Saying the word "Stop!" further breaks your automatic habit pattern of worry. Then reading the Word of God aloud becomes the positive substitute for worry. If you are in a group of people and begin to worry, follow the same procedure, only do it silently.

The woman who shared in the class said that on the first day of her experiment, she took out the card twenty times during the day. Five days later, she took it out only three times.

She said happily, "For the first time in my life, I have the hope that my worrisome thinking can be chased out of my life!"

Freedom from worry is possible! It requires practicing, challenging and replacing your self-talk, and being diligent in applying God's Word to your life. Remember, practice means repetitive behavior. If you fail, don't give up. You may have practiced worrying for many years, and now you need to practice consistently the application of Scripture over a long period in order to completely establish a new, worry-free pattern.

We all experience negative thoughts, at times. That's normal. If we're functioning well at the time, we may tell ourselves, That's not reality. That's a distortion.

When Depression Clouds Our Thoughts

When you're depressed, what type of thoughts do you have? Do any in the list below reflect your thinking? What's the correlation between the thoughts and any depression you're experiencing?

The authors of *The Mindful Way Through Depression* suggested that the following are common automatic thoughts of depressed people:

1. I feel like I'm up against the world.
2. I'm no good.
3. Why can't I ever succeed?
4. No one understands me.
5. I've let people down.
6. I don't think I can go on.
7. I wish I were a better person.

8. I'm so weak.

9. My life's not going the way I want it to.

10. I'm so disappointed in myself.

11. Nothing feels good anymore.

12. I can't stand this anymore.

13. I can't get started.

14. What's wrong with me?

15. I wish I were somewhere else.

16. I can't get things together.

17. I hate myself.

18. I'm worthless.

19. I wish I could just disappear.

20. What's the matter with me?

21. I'm a loser.

22. My life is a mess.

23. I'm a failure.

24. I'll never make it.

25. I feel so helpless.

26. Something has to change.

27. There must be something wrong with me.

28. My future is bleak.

29. It's just not worth it.

30. I can't finish anything.[7]

Scripture has much to say about our thoughts and emotions, sometimes directly and sometimes through the experience of a person. Jeremiah the prophet gives us a practical example. He was depressed. We don't know all the reasons, but thoughts were part of them.

He believed God had caused his despondency. He said,

> I am the man who has seen affliction
> by the rod of his wrath.
> He has driven me away and made me walk
>   in darkness rather than light;
> indeed, he has turned his hand against me
>   again and again, all day long.
>   (Lam. 3:1–3 NIV)

As many do, he experienced physical symptoms as well:

> He has made my skin and my flesh grow old
>   and has broken my bones. (Lam. 3:4 NIV)

He felt trapped. He didn't see any hope:

> He has besieged me and surrounded me
>   with bitterness and hardship.
> He has made me dwell in darkness
>   like those long dead. (Lam. 3:5–6 NIV)

And he continued to blame God:

> He has walled me in so I cannot escape;
>   he has weighed me down with chains.
> Even when I call out or cry for help,
>   he shuts out my prayer.
> He has barred my way with blocks of stone;
>   he has made my paths crooked.
>   (Lam. 3:7–9 NIV)

He continues by thinking everyone is out to get him:

> Like a bear lying in wait,
>   like a lion in hiding,
> he dragged me from the path and mangled me
>   and left me without help.
> He drew his bow
>   and made me the target for his arrows.
> He pierced my heart
>   with arrows from his quiver.
> I became the laughingstock of all my people;
>   they mock me in song all day long.
> He has filled me with bitter herbs
>   and sated me with gall. (Lam. 3:10–15 NIV)

His despair is total:

> He has broken my teeth with gravel;
>   he has trampled me in the dust.
> I have been deprived of peace;
>   I have forgotten what prosperity is.
> So I say, "My splendor is gone
>   and all that I had hoped from the LORD."
>   (Lam. 3:16–18 NIV)

But notice a major insight in these next verses:

> I remember my affliction and my wandering,
>   the bitterness and the gall.
> I well remember them,
>   and my soul is downcast within me.
>   (Lam. 3:19–20 NIV)

The Amplified translation states in verse 20, "My soul has them continually in remembrance."

The word *continually* doesn't mean now and then—it means it's constant. It doesn't let up. Look at what he's been thinking about—anyone would feel miserable. It's all negative.

But in verse 21, we see a reversal—a change in his thinking:

> Yet this I call to mind
> and therefore I have hope. (NIV)

The phrase "call to mind" is what we all need to do. It's a remembering. It's shifting from looking at the worst of everything, to focusing on the positive. And in this case, his hope is in who God is and what he does. Look at verses 22–24:

> Because of the LORD's great love we are not consumed,
> for his compassions never fail.
> They are new every morning;
> great is your faithfulness.
> I say to myself, "The LORD is my portion;
> therefore I will wait for him." (NIV)

We all could follow this example and ask, What is it I need to call to mind?

Perhaps, like Jeremiah, it's remembering God's blessings, his work, and who he is.

The amount of love and acceptance that God has for you cannot be measured nor comprehended. When you're depressed, search for the blessings that are being overshadowed or ignored.

This isn't denying difficulties, but just bringing a balance into your thought life. Negative thinking can lead a person into depression. And when we're depressed, we continue to think more and more negatively, which reinforces the depression.

Many of your emotional reactions depend on the story you tell yourself. With some people, their thoughts sound like a newscaster telling the story of their life. They have a running commentary going on in their mind that intercepts experiences.

If we're objective in our story and give ourselves the benefit of the doubt, we may feel little or no reaction about events. If we're down on ourselves in our self-talk or already a bit depressed, our mind may take off with more toxic thoughts, and we end up feeling worse—depressed, angry, guilty, or lonely.

Remember in an earlier chapter we saw how we ruminate on our thoughts. Well, the link between rumination and depression is quite strong. We are more vulnerable to depression when we ruminate, and when this continues, it's difficult to overcome the depression.

If this is your problem, the authors of *The Depression Cure* have suggested that your first step in the right direction is to be alert.[8] Monitor your thinking. Not just in a random fashion, but regularly, such as every hour. Use a prompt to remind yourself, such as an alarm on your cell phone. You may want to keep a journal, recording how long you ruminate on an issue, and what your mood was during that time.

Does this take some effort? Yes, but not much. Does it cause you to pay close attention to your thinking? Yes. And by doing this, you'll discover what's going on in your mind, giving you the chance to catch it early and take steps to change.

Some people believe their ruminating is helpful. They say, "If I just spend a bit more time thinking, it will help me." It won't.

Don't believe me? Try this: When you catch yourself ruminating on a worry, allow yourself ten minutes to continue. Set a timer, and when it goes off, stop. Think about what you accomplished. Probably nothing.[9]

Thoughts and depression are closely connected. In *Moving Beyond Depression*, Dr. Gregory Lantz said:

> It is part of the human condition that negative thoughts seem to flow easier than logical and more positive ones. An overactive brain can take a small incident and quickly inflate it into a major crisis. If this pattern is repeated often enough, the person becomes swept away in this mental torrent, unable to find the footholds they need to return to the solid ground of common sense and reality. When the flow of thoughts slows down, the person is able to better realize the truth and maintain a grip on their probabilities.
>
> If a person is naturally pessimistic, inclined toward runaway thoughts, depression is often the result. The person who feels powerless to control his or her thoughts assumes that the worst that can happen soon will. This focus on disaster does not allow the person to keep optimism, hope, or joy in his or her sights for very long, if at all. Negative self-talk and the grim atmosphere of a foul mood fuel this fatalistic mental spiral.[10]

When you are depressed, you have a chemical imbalance in your brain. Thoughts trigger emotions, which dump an overload of stress chemicals into the brain. There is a chemical consequence in the brain for every thought we think.

Depression can be short-circuited temporarily by the brain-switching process. It's a way of restoring the chemical balance. The thoughts that create depression connect with one's memory banks, which have emotional associations.

In *The Depression Cure*, Ilardi writes:

> There's evidence that depression can leave a toxic imprint on the brain. It can etch its way into our neural circuitry—including the brain's stress response system—and make it much easier for the brain to fall back into another episode of depression down the road. This helps explain a puzzling fact: It normally takes a high level of life stress to trigger someone's *first* episode of depression, but later relapse episodes sometimes come totally out of the blue. It seems that once the brain has learned how to operate in depression mode, it can find its way back there with much less prompting.
>
> Fortunately, though, we can heal from the damage of depression. All it takes is several months of complete recovery for much of the toxic imprint on the brain to be erased [or overridden].[11]

In brainswitching, you choose a new thought that's neutral or nonsense. This thought doesn't trigger the same emotional, and resulting chemical, responses in the brain.

Instead, the new thought actually creates activity in the neocortex—the thinking part of the brain. Depressive thoughts activate the subcortex, the feeling part of the brain.

We have the choice of using either the subcortex (feeling portion) or the neocortex (thinking portion) region of our brain. Remember, your mind will move in the direction of the most current and dominant thought.

You can make a thought dominant by saying it over and over again. Even repeatedly saying, "I am depressed" has an effect upon your depression. And when you're depressed you tend to act in a way that reinforces your depression.

You may look depressed. You think defeatist, depressive thoughts. When you're depressed you're letting your mind tell you what to feel, think, and do.

The author of *BrainSwitch Out of Depression* suggests that we can choose thoughts that will bring us out of depression. Practically anything that is repeated again and again will work. Remember the importance of repetition?[12]

It could be a nursery rhyme. Sounds ridiculous, right? Well, I've seen the results firsthand.

People have kicked out depression simply by repeating phrases such as "blue cat" or "purple dogs" or "pink frog." It's true!

These new phrases directly initiate activity in the brain, away from the parts that respond to depressed thinking. The new words activate neurons in the thinking part of the brain. Activity in the feeling portion slows. Stress chemicals being poured into the brain diminish.

You might choose to short-circuit the cycle of thinking that leads to depression by repeating the phrase, "Yes, praise God." Or you might pray for yourself or someone else. You could also say, "I can do this!" Any affirmations will work.[13]

You also can improve mood and eliminate worrying by following these tips:

Don't spend so much time thinking. Begin experiencing the world without the running commentary in your mind.

Don't take your thoughts as the gospel truth. Think of them like the clouds, drifting across the sky. At times they're there, and then they're gone. They have no permanence.

Look at each day as a new day, disconnected from the past and future, so you can experience what God has in store for you.

Pay attention to your thought life. Are your thoughts drifting, or are you choosing to focus them? Remember, you're in charge—of your thoughts *and* actions.

Accept the way things are right now, and look for the positive in this moment, rather than assuming positive things are only possible in the future.

If your thinking begins moving toward depression, interrupt your thinking process. Go back and restart. This time, put in realistic thoughts. Rewind your story and write a new ending. Determine a new outcome.[14]

There are numerous causes for depression. For more information on depression, I would encourage you to read *Breaking Through Depression* by Donald Hall; *BrainSwitch Out of Depression* by A. B. Curtiss; and *The Depression Cure* by Dr. Stephen Ilardi.

Reflect and Remember

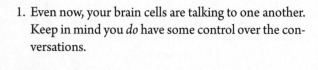

1. Even now, your brain cells are talking to one another. Keep in mind you *do* have some control over the conversations.

2. What are five issues you tend to worry about?

   a.

   b.

   c.

   d.

   e.

3. At what times do you tend to worry?

   _____

   _____

   _____

4. What's your plan to overcome the worry in your life?

5. Look up Psalm 37:1–9. What are four alternatives to fretting that the psalmist suggests? What do these mean to you?

6. What are some of the "yeah-buts" you tend to use? What can you say instead?

7. Which of the automatic thoughts on the list reflect your thoughts?

8. What thoughts would help you, if you called them to mind?

_____

_____

9. What new phrase, statement, or strategy will you use to counter depressive thoughts?

_____

_____

New Thoughts

If you knew Cheryl five years ago, you might not recognize her today. She's settled, secure, and has a smile on her face that's genuine.

Five years ago, she was fretful, angry, and upset much of the time. Something happened. There was a change.

If you were to ask Cheryl what happened, she'd tell you with a smile on her face. You'd hear two things: One, she developed a new "mind diet"; and two, she engaged in following the teaching of Scripture, especially the admonition to "practice." She had a new direction for her life. But what exactly did she do?

Cheryl compared it to navigating an airplane. There are three instruments every plane must have—the compass, the altimeter, and the artificial horizon. The latter instrument tells the pilot which way is up and which way is down.

When you fly into clouds and can't see anything, nothing in your body will tell you which way is "up" and which is "down." But the artificial horizon will.

The Guidance and Instruction of Scripture

Many people use their thoughts to guide them, to give them direction. We need something more than this because we really don't always have a good sense of direction within us. The prophet Jeremiah confirmed this: "I know, O Lord, that the way of human beings is not in their control, that mortals as they walk cannot direct their steps" (Jer. 10:23 NRSV). We need God's Word.

Scripture instructs us about our thoughts, our imagination, and our self-talk—and how to take control. Remember earlier, when we mentioned that the words *think, thought*, and *mind* are used over three hundred times in the Scriptures? God is aware of our struggles and our need for strength. When we give ourselves to God, he begins a work on our minds.

Isaiah 26:3–4 says, "You will keep in perfect peace him whose mind is steadfast, because he trusts in you. Trust in the LORD forever, for the LORD, the LORD, is the Rock eternal" (NIV). If you express this promise aloud every day, it will change your thoughts. It can be rephrased in this way: "God, you will give me perfect peace, and keep me in perfect and constant peace, when my mind is fixed upon you. I commit myself to you—to lean on you and hope in you. I trust in you." Expressed again and again this passage will begin to penetrate your mind.

In Philippians 2:5, we read, "Let the same mind be in you that was in Christ Jesus" (NRSV). The verse also could be translated, "Have the same attitude toward one another as you have toward Christ Jesus," or "Be disposed toward one another as you are toward Christ Jesus." The verb "disposed" suggests more than logic; it suggests an attitude.

In *The Mind of Christ*, Dennis Kinlaw writes this:

Paul again uses the same word [*mind*] in Romans 8, where he says, "Those who live according to the flesh and controlled by its unholy desires, set their minds on *and* pursue those things which gratify the flesh. But those who live according to the Spirit *and* [controlled by the desires] of the Spirit, set their minds on *and* seek those things that gratify the (Holy) Spirit" (v. 5, AMP). He is not merely talking about a philosophical system. The word suggests the desires of a person's heart. We get a similar connotation in Colossians 3:2–3, where Paul says, "Set your minds on things that are above, not in things that are on earth, for you have died, and your life is hidden with Christ in God."

To have "the mind of Christ" is to have his perspective, his attitude, his affections and priorities. The Bible calls us to have the mind of Christ within us, rather than merely learning how to imitate him. We are challenged to allow his mind to guide our lives. This is such a marvelous thing that we can scarcely comprehend it. The Gospels challenge us to think the way Christ thinks. The New Testament Epistles emphasize that we should expect "the mind of Christ" to be given to us.[1]

People sometimes ask, "Is it possible to get a brain or mind transplant?" We all laugh . . . at first. But the idea isn't without appeal. It sometimes seems it would be easier to start over with a clean slate, rather than continue enduring the turmoil that occurs inside our minds, or go through all the work it takes to change these entrenched patterns. But wait! According to Scripture, it *is* possible to have a change in our mind.

> Under the controlling power of the Holy Spirit, a believer can direct his thoughts and energies toward God.

"Do not be conformed to this world (this age), [fashioned after and adapted to its external, superficial customs], but be transformed (changed) by the [entire] renewal of your mind [by its new ideals and new attitude], so that you may prove [for yourselves] what is the good and acceptable and perfect will of God, even the thing which is good and acceptable and perfect [in His sight for you]" (Rom. 12:2 AMP).

The renewal here is the spirit of the mind. Under the controlling power of the Holy Spirit, a believer can direct his thoughts and energies toward God. The renewing of the mind is the adjustment of the person's thinking and outlook on life so that these conform to the mind of God.

We want our mind to be focused on Christlike thoughts, as we're instructed in Colossians 3:1–2: "If then you have been raised with Christ, seek the things that are above, where Christ is, seated at the right hand of God. *Set your minds on things* that are above, not on things that are on earth" (ESV, emphasis added). The phrase "set your mind on" means to think on, or focus on.

Ephesians 1:18 speaks of "having the eyes of your heart enlightened" (ESV) or "having the eyes of your heart flooded with light" (AMP).

Ephesians 4:22–23 admonishes: "Strip yourselves of your former nature [put off and discard your old unrenewed self] which characterized your previous manner of life and becomes corrupt through lusts and desires that spring from delusion; And be constantly renewed in the spirit of your mind [having a fresh mental and spiritual attitude]" (AMP).

And 1 Peter 1:13 instructs: "So brace up your minds; be sober (circumspect, morally alert); set your hope wholly and unchangeably on the grace (divine favor) that is coming to you when Jesus Christ (the Messiah) is revealed" (AMP).

God's Plan for Our Minds

God does have a plan for our minds. He has an ideal for it. Six times the New Testament describes or implies what a Christian's mind is to be like.

First, it is to be *alive*.

The first reference to how the mind should be is in Romans 8:6: "For the mind set on the flesh is death, but the mind set on the Spirit is life and peace" (NASB).

When we invite Jesus Christ into our lives, we have a new life. We come alive. We show this new life by choices we make. It's a major adjustment for many. We're now faced with choices of what we think about, what we dwell on, what we put into our mind, what we say, and so on. I've heard some say, "After I invited Jesus into my life, I felt alive for the first time in my life."

Think about it. Take time to sit and reflect: Are you still struggling with the old thinking pattern, with clutter in your mind? Or is there a sense of being alive in your mind and thought life?

Fears can be changed into feelings of rest and security. That's being alive.

Second, God's standard for our mind is also that it's *peaceful*. We read, again in Romans 8:6, "The mind of the [Holy] Spirit is life and [soul] peace" (AMP).

> You and I have choices as to what we focus on in our thought life.

You and I have choices as to what we focus on in our thought life. Paul said, "For those who are according to the flesh and are controlled by its unholy desires set their minds on and pursue those things which gratify the flesh, but those who are according to the Spirit and are controlled by the desires of the Spirit set their minds on and seek those things which gratify the [Holy] Spirit" (Rom. 8:5 AMP). You and I *set* our minds. That's our work. The result of doing this is peace, which is God's work.

Third, God wants us to stay *focused*. "But [now] I am fearful, lest that even as the serpent beguiled Eve by his cunning, so your minds may be corrupted and seduced from wholehearted and sincere and pure devotion to Christ" (2 Cor. 11:3 AMP). Distractions are all around us, and our thoughts can drift and lead us astray. It takes effort to stay focused.

The fourth characteristic God wants our minds to reflect is *lowliness*. The Bible instructs, "Do nothing out of selfish ambition or vain conceit, but in humility consider others better than yourselves" (Phil. 2:3 NIV). How we think about ourselves determines how we treat others.

One way to gain a realistic estimate of who *we* are is to look at the attributes of God and Jesus. Who am I in relationship to them? Thinking about that puts me in my proper place and position.

Unfortunately, some of us become legends in our own minds, and we expect others to see us in that same way. I've run into many who think too highly of themselves, and expect others to see them in the same light. That's not having a lowly attitude. Our example and model is Jesus.

Let each of you esteem and look upon and be concerned for not [merely] his own interests, but also each for the interests of others. Let this same attitude and purpose and [humble] mind be in you which was in Christ Jesus: [Let Him be your example in humility:] Who, although being essentially one with God and in the form of God [possessing the fullness of the attributes which make God God], did not think this equality with God was a thing to be eagerly grasped or retained, But stripped Himself [of all privileges and rightful dignity], so as to assume the guise of a servant (slave), in that He became like men and was born a human being. And after He had appeared in human form, He abased and humbled Himself [still further] and carried His obedience to the extreme of death, even the death of the cross! Therefore [because He stooped so low] God has highly exalted Him and has freely bestowed on Him the name that is above every name. (Phil. 2:4–9 AMP)

If we followed this, perhaps our self-talk would move from "I deserve this" to "I appreciate whatever occurs, and I'm thankful." We'd move from trying to elevate ourselves, to thinking about how we could elevate others.

A *pure* mind is the fifth characteristic God wants for us. Titus 1:15 says, "To the pure, all things are pure, but to those who are corrupted and do not believe, nothing is pure. In fact, both their minds and consciences are corrupted" (NIV).

Having a pure mind is a good goal. But on our own, it's difficult. Many of our thoughts quickly move to wanting something that doesn't belong to us, whether it's another person, or someone else's possessions, position, or power. The issue of lust is a battleground for many. Temptations can consume and control us.

Keeping our minds pure might be as simple as making a plan. Plans help us take charge of problems. To keep a pure mind, we need to plan (in writing) our response to temptation. We need to identify thoughts that tempt us, then make a plan to defeat those thoughts, before they get us into trouble.

Write what you will do the next time you think that way. Plan how you will stop or switch your thoughts. What Scriptures can you memorize and use at this time?

One that's helped me throughout my life is, "No temptation has seized you except what is common to man. And God is faithful; he will not let you be tempted beyond what you can bear. But when you are tempted, he will also provide a way out so that you can stand up under it" (1 Cor. 10:13 NIV). Time and time again, especially when I was a young man, the Holy Spirit brought this passage to mind and kept me from making the wrong choice.

The last characteristic of a Christian's mind is that it's *sensitive* and *responsive*. A believer is one who is open to learning. There's a spiritual sensitivity to God. In Luke 24:45, we see that Jesus "opened their minds so they could understand the Scriptures" (NIV).

As Jesus opened the minds of the disciples to learn, he opens our minds. If we're going to see a change in our mind, we need to be responsive and have open minds to what God has for us.[2]

Change comes through understanding his Word. T. W. Hunt, in *The Mind of Christ*, describes it this way:

> As the Father is to the Son, so Christ is to us. He imitated the Father; we imitate Christ. He saw the activity of the Father; we pay close attention to the known earthly activity of Jesus (and, for that matter, also to His present activity). He heard from the Father; we must hear from Him. The Father taught Him; He teaches us. He could do nothing independently of the Father; we cannot function independently of Him. He was very close to the Father; we must

remain close to Him. Pray that God will make you more sensitive to Him.[3]

Toxic Thoughts about Oneself

Over the years, I've asked men and women to give me a description of their mind and thought life. I've heard responses like:

"My mind and my thoughts are troubled."

"My mind and my thoughts are in turmoil."

"My mind never seems to shut down. It seems to run constantly."

"I wish my mind and my thoughts were kinder . . . at least toward me. I never seem to cut myself any slack."

"Negative—just plain negative. I'm really hard on myself."

These men and women are describing conflict. But it doesn't have to be this way.

In *ReThink Your Life*, Stan Toler writes,

It's so important that the Bible uses warfare-type language when discussing it in 2 Corinthians 10:3–5: "For though we live in the world, we do not wage war as the world does. The weapons we fight with are not the weapons of the world. On the contrary, they have divine power to demolish strongholds. We demolish arguments and every pretension that sets itself up against the knowledge of God, and we take captive every thought to make it obedient to Christ."

There's something powerful in the idea of taking captive every thought.[4]

It may help you to answer this question: Is my mind my ally or adversary? It's not a trick question!

A mind filled with negative or toxic thoughts toward yourself and others will keep your life in turmoil. This is why we need the stability of God's Word.

By this point in your reading I'm sure you're aware of the negative thoughts or comments that go through your mind.

Jean, a woman in counseling, said, "For the past fifteen years I've been struggling with what I say to myself. I've begun to realize that I'm my own worst enemy. Others tell me I'm gifted and capable. Perhaps, but it doesn't show in my schooling or at work. I do all right, but not what others say I'm capable of doing. When a challenge arises I tell myself, 'I can't do this,' or 'That's too hard. What if I try and fail? What will everyone else think of me? Others will know I'm not capable.' So I find ways *not* to try. I couldn't stand it if others knew how inept I am."

Did you hear Jean's negative self-talk? Go back over her story and underline every statement you believe is negative. Then using the space provided below, write some of the negative statements you make to yourself about yourself. You're the only one besides God who will see these. And remember, he already knows them.

1. _____
2. _____
3. _____
4. _____
5. _____
6. _____

It could be upsetting to actually see these statements in writing. The longer we've had these thoughts about ourselves, the more we've trained ourselves to believe them. We see them as the truth. We tend to believe them, because we think, If they came into my mind automatically they must be true. But they're not.

True Thoughts about Oneself

I can suggest a number of positive thoughts you could use to replace your toxic thoughts about yourself. But it's not what I think that's important. It's what God says. He is the ultimate source of truth. Once again look at Scripture.

Here's a sample of what God's Word says:

I am accepted	
John 1:12	I am God's child.
Romans 5:1	I have been justified.
1 Corinthians 6:19–20	I have been bought with a price and I belong to God.
Ephesians 1:3–8	I have been chosen by God and adopted as his child.
Colossians 1:13–14	I have been redeemed and forgiven of all my sins.
Colossians 2:9–10	I am complete in Christ.
I am secure	
Romans 8:28	I am assured that God works for my good in all circumstances.
Philippians 1:6	I am confident that God will complete the good work he started in me.
2 Timothy 1:7	I have not been given a spirit of fear, but a spirit of power, love, and a sound mind.

I am significant	
1 Corinthians 3:16	I am God's temple.
Ephesians 2:10	I am God's workmanship.
Philippians 4:13	I can do all things through Christ, who strengthens me.

How can you fashion your thoughts to meet God's standard? I like what Stan Toler says:

> As Christians, we are to surrender our mind so that Jesus becomes lord of the way we think. Now, surrendering our minds doesn't mean that we stop thinking. Not at all. Christians can and should be among the most logical, rational, intellectually curious people in the world. Remember that God created our minds, and he expects us to use them to the best of our abilities!
>
> ... Surrendering your mind to Christ *does* mean to choose Jesus as your mentor or teacher, to trust his wisdom as a guide for your life. It means to trust that his way of understanding and making sense of the world is true, accurate, and sufficient. If you choose to believe what Jesus believes, to order your life according to the principles he teaches, and to offer your life in his service, then you are surrendering your mind to Jesus.
>
> Learning to think the way Jesus thinks doesn't happen in an evening or a weekend. Just as soldiers go through basic training to prepare themselves for military service, Christians must submit themselves to training for Kingdom service.[5]

Challenging Self-Talk to Reflect Truth

Would you like Jesus to become Lord of the way you think? Most would. So, how can you change your pattern of thinking?

How can you surrender your mind? It's a cooperative venture. The new content really doesn't come from you alone. It comes from God and his Word and the Holy Spirit working in your life. It can be a slow process, and it does involve effort on your part. Here are several suggestions:

We've talked about challenging self-talk before. Does it feel strange to challenge your thoughts?

We're used to seeing challenges in sporting events. In tennis matches, the line judge makes a call on where the ball landed. If the player who ended up on the wrong side of the call disagrees, he challenges the decision. With instant replays we're able to see whether the call was correct or not.

Football coaches are now able to challenge the ruling of a play, and often the decision is reversed. These challenges are somewhat new in the world of sports, but they've made the results much more accurate.

You and I have the same freedom and opportunity to challenge the validity and accuracy of what's occurring in our thought life. The same process of challenging and evaluating your beliefs can be applied to your toxic or hot thoughts.

As you challenge your toxic or hot thought, keep these summary questions at the forefront:

What was my thought?

What is the evidence that supports it?

What is the evidence that doesn't support it?

What do I do now?

Now, you'll want to create a list of positive truthful statements about yourself. How? One way is to take a negative thought and rewrite it so it's an affirming truthful expression. Create at least six or eight of these.

Negative thought: (Example: I'm fat.)

Rewritten as a positive: (Example: I've made progress recently in my efforts to eat healthier, and that's bound to have positive results on my health and weight, as I stick with it.)

If you're like many of us, you've spent years in training your mind. The constant repetition of negative thoughts created a groove of negative thinking in your brain.

Think about it. If you only had that thought once, there's no permanent effect. But what if you thought it five thousand times over the years? I've driven on a dirt road when it was first created. It was smooth and flat. Months later, my vehicle bounced over ruts where tires had rolled over the same path thousands of times.

Now it's time to begin your brain-retraining program. Your goal is to develop a new, healthy, groove-filled road with truthful thoughts. These are the steps that will help you reach your goal of making peace with your mind.

Each day select a statement of positive truth about yourself from your list. (It's also important to add at least two new statements about yourself each week for a month.)

Then, select one of the scriptural truths from the list in the preceding "True Thoughts about Oneself." That will help you build a new foundation in your mind to draw upon, as you relate to yourself and others.

This will take constant practice and time—more time than you can imagine or even want. But in doing this, you'll also be following scriptural teaching. Paul said,

> For the rest, brethren, whatever is true, whatever is worthy of reverence and is honorable and seemly, whatever is just, whatever is pure, whatever is lovely and lovable, whatever is kind and winsome and gracious, if there is any virtue and excellence, if there is anything worthy of praise, think on and weigh and take account of these things [*fix your minds on them*]. *Practice* what you have learned and received and heard and seen in me, and model your way of living on it, and the God of peace (of untroubled, undisturbed well-being) will be with you. (Phil. 4:8–9 AMP, emphasis added)

Notice the word Paul used—*practice*. Haven't we said this all before? Practice is repetitive behavior—again and again and again. Paul is saying, "Take action. Do something about your worry and negative thinking!" The Message translation says it this way: "Summing it all up, friends, I'd say you'll do best by filling your minds and meditating on things true, noble, reputable, authentic, compelling, gracious—the best, not the worst; the beautiful, not the ugly; things to praise, not things to curse. Put into practice what you learned from me, what you heard and saw and realized."

Jot down both statements—the positive truth about yourself and the scriptural truth—and carry it with you all day.

The more you read and say these statements, the more they become a part of your life. Think about it this way—you won't really be doing anything new, except changing the message. You've been making statements about yourself for years, and what you're doing now is replacing the critical, toxic statements with truth.

As I've said before, this will take consistent effort on your part. But it's worth the time and energy. The scriptural promise of a more peaceful mind was meant for you.

I've already shared the importance of expressing yourself aloud. Several times a day (each hour would be better), read aloud the two statements you've selected. That's right, out loud with a strong voice. (It's best to do this when no one else is around.)

The more you do this, the easier it will become, and the more you'll believe what you're saying. It's one thing to think it, and see it in your mind, and say it there. But when it's audible, when you hear it in your own voice, the new thought gains a greater foothold. Numerous authors and therapists have suggested these approaches over the years. The authors of *The Worry Free Life* call these Christian affirmations, and prescribe something called The Mirror Technique:

> Stand in front of a mirror and try to convince the person in the mirror how important it is for him or her to believe your Christian Affirmation. You need to point out to the person in the mirror the significance of Christian Affirmation. This works best if you can become emotionally involved in trying to influence the mirror image to believe what you are saying. Pretend you are an actress or actor playing a part. Use every available acting skill you can think of to convince

this image how outstanding and sensational this Christian Affirmation is. Do this several times a day.[6]

One of the approaches that's been helpful for those who have experienced trauma is writing out their story . . . repeatedly. It works like this. Take a piece of paper and divide it into three columns:

Positive Truth

Objection

Confirmation of the Scriptural Truth

In the first column write the words you've selected for the day. Because these thoughts are new and perhaps foreign to your way of thinking, you'll probably experience rebuttals or objections to the truth. When this occurs write it down in the Objection column. In the last column, write your rebuttal or challenge to this objection. It could be as basic as a simple rebuttal to the negative statement.

Once you've completed that, return to the first column and write your words for the day once again. When an objection or rebuttal surfaces again, write it down and then write your rebuttal and challenge it once again. Continue this process until the objection or rebuttals have stopped coming to your mind.

Some have found it helpful to stay with these initial truths for several days. Then when you feel ready, select a new positive truth and scriptural truth, and repeat this same process until your objection/rebuttal doesn't occur. In time your view of yourself and others will change.[7]

Here's an example of this process:

TRUTH	OBJECTION	TRUTH
I am highly valued by God. I am really worthwhile.	Who says you are? Others don't believe this and deep down you don't.	God is the one who says this. That's all I need. It's his greatest gift; I'm highly valued.

This is not a one-week or one-month activity. You may need to use this for years. We all have an innate bent toward negative thinking. And it takes time to change our thought patterns.

As you work, you'll probably find it's more effective to identify your positive thought first, and bring it into your mind alongside the negative, rather than attempt to evict the negative first and then replace it with the positive and scriptural truths.

But the next step is critical. Over the past two decades there's been a change in the thinking of educators and therapists. What's been found to work best is to focus on what's working or going well in a person's life or a relationship, rather than what's wrong or isn't working. It's not as much problem-oriented as it is solution-oriented.

In parenting, the emphasis is on catching a child doing something right, rather than wrong. Parents are trained to focus on positive behavior rather than negative.

You probably know where this is heading. As you work on changing your thinking, give yourself credit for any improvement, and keep your eyes focused there. Catch yourself thinking correctly. And praise yourself for it.

With a negative thinking pattern in place it would be natural to let that overrule positive changes. Just concentrate on what's working, watch it expand, and thank God for your progress. In time, you'll have succeeded in making changes that will last.

You may be thinking: I've come to the end of the book. Well, maybe. Maybe not.

The value of any book is the impact it has on our lives. It could be that you selected this volume because you were curious, or you just wanted to make some quick changes in your thought life. Well, there's not a quick fix in any book. But there are some life-changing suggestions in this one, if you internalize them, practice them, and submit to God's guidance in your life.

We've explored the power of imagination, fantasy, self-talk, core thoughts, automatic thoughts, toxic thoughts, and wandering thoughts. I've shown you the value of identifying thoughts that affect your life in a negative way, and I've shown you how to reformulate thoughts with turn-around power. You now know how to create new thoughts and make them part of your thinking, by writing them, saying them aloud, and practicing exercises that make them take up residence in your mind permanently.

Perhaps your next step will be to reread this book. You're almost sure to discover something new you missed on your first time through.

Then, it may be time to identify the changes you've begun, and practice, practice, practice.

It would also be helpful to look again at the Scriptures that address the mind. Memorize them. Experience them . . . and discover a new freedom!

In Jeremiah 33:3, God's Word promises: "Call to me and I will answer you and tell you great and unsearchable things you do not know" (NIV).

And we rejoice, knowing good things lie ahead. For in Jeremiah 29:11, we hear the wonderful news: "'For I know the plans I have for you,' declares the LORD, 'plans to prosper you and not to harm you, plans to give you hope and a future'" (NIV).

Reflect and Remember

1. Describe how you allow God to give you perfect peace.

   _____

   _____

   _____

2. If I were to have the mind of Christ, I would . . .

   _____

   _____

   _____

   _____

3. Describe a time in which you felt your mind was renewed.

   _____

   _____

   _____

4. Which of the six examples of how our mind is supposed to be do you need to work on the most?

_____

_____

5. What word describes your thought life?

_____

_____

Notes

CHAPTER 1 My Mind Is Filled with Thoughts!

1. Adapted from Dr. Caroline Leaf, *Who Switched Off My Brain?* (Dallas: Switch on Your Brain, Inc., 2008), 3–4.

2. Archibald Hart, *Habits of the Mind* (Dallas: Word, 1996), 5.

3. Ibid., 6.

4. Don Colbert, *Deadly Emotions* (Nashville: Thomas Nelson, 2003), 183.

5. Daniel Amen, *Change Your Brain, Change Your Life* (New York: Three Rivers Press, 1999), 56–58.

6. Leaf, *Who Switched Off My Brain?*, 4.

7. Colbert, *Deadly Emotions*, 24–27.

8. Leaf, *Who Switched Off My Brain?*, 9–10.

9. Ibid., introduction.

10. Charles Swindoll, *Come Before Winter* (Portland: Multnomah, 1985), 29.

CHAPTER 2 Where Do Thoughts Come From?

1. Michael Gurian, *The Wonder of Boys* (New York: Tarcher/Putnam, 1996), 15.

2. Gary Emery, *Own Your Own Life* (New York: New American Library, 1982), 9.

3. Adapted from Dallas Willard, *Renovation of the Heart* (Colorado Springs: NavPress, 2002), 90; and David Matthew, *Sound Mind* (Ringgold, GA: Harvestime, 1987).

4. Dennis Greenberger and Christine P. Padesky, *Mind Over Mood* (New York: The Guilford Press, 1995), 51.

5. Shad Helmstetter, *The Self-Talk Solution* (New York: Pocket Books, 1987), 49–51.

6. Ibid., adapted, 85–89.

7. Mark Williams, John Teasdale, Zendel Segal, and Jon Kabat-Zinn, *The Mindful Way through Depression* (New York: Guilford Press, 2007), 167–69.

8. Peter McWilliams, *You Can't Afford the Luxury of a Negative Thought* (Santa Monica, CA: Prelude Press, 1995), 31–32.

9. Williams et al., *Mindful Way*, 177.

10. Robert W. Firestone, Lisa Firestone, and Joyce Callett, *Conquering Your Critical Inner Voice* (Oakland, CA: New Harbinger Publications, 2002), 25.

CHAPTER 3 The Gift of Imagination

1. Edgar Allan Poe, *Eleonora* (Charleston, SC: BookSurge, 2004), 1.

2. A. W. Tozer, "The Value of a Sanctified Imagination," in Warren Wiersbe, *Developing a Christian Imagination* (Wheaton: Victor, 1995), 212.

3. Vincent Collins, *Me, Myself and You* (St. Meinard, IN: Abbey Press, 1974), 30.

4. Alexander Whyte: As quoted by Hannah Hurnard in *Winged Life* (Wheaton, IL: Tyndale, 1978).

5. Stan Toler, *ReThink Your Life* (Indianapolis: Wesleyan Publishing House, 2008), 30–31.

6. Adapted from Matthew, *Sound Mind*, 101, 103.

7. Ibid.

CHAPTER 4 Core Beliefs—The Source of Your Thoughts

1. Adapted from Shad Helmstetter, *What to Say When You Talk to Your Self* (New York: Pocket Books, 1982), 20–21.

2. Byron Brown, *Soul Without Shame* (Boston: Shambhala, 1999), 14.

3. Dave Ziegler, *Traumatic Experience and the Brain* (Phoenix: Acacia Publishing, 2002), adapted, 42–43.

4. H. Norman Wright, *A Dad-Shaped Hole in My Heart* (Grand Rapids: Baker, 2005), 62–65.

5. Greenberger and Padesky, *Mind Over Mood*, 130–47.

CHAPTER 5 Self-Talk—Taking More Control

1. Edward E. Moody Jr., *First Aid for Emotional Hurts* (Nashville: Randall House, 2008), 96–97; S. Nolen-Hoekssma and C. Davis, "'Thanks for Sharing That,' Ruminators and Their Social Support Networks," *Journal of Personality and Social Psychology*, 77, 4 (1999), 801–14.

2. Jeffrey Bernstein and Susan Magee, *Why Can't You Read My Mind?* (Philadelphia: Da Capo Press, 2004), 11–12.

3. Penelope Russvanoff, *When Am I Going to Be Happy?* (New York: Bantam, 1989), 6.

4. Bernstein and Magee, *Why Can't You Read My Mind?*, 57–60.

5. Williams et al., *Mindful Way*, 76–87.

6. Laura Davis, *I Thought We'd Never Speak Again* (New York: Harper, 2003), 7.

7. A. B. Curtiss, *BrainSwitch Out of Depression* (San Diego: Healthworks Clinic Press, 2006), adapted, 34–35.

8. Ibid., adapted, 37–38.

9. James J. Asher, *Brainswitching* (Los Gatos, CA: Sky Oaks Productions, 1988), 50.

CHAPTER 6 Igniting Change—What's Holding You Back?

1. Daniel Rutley, *Escaping Emotional Entrapment* (Lakeland, FL: Pax Publishing, 2001), adapted, 64.

2. Swindoll, *Come Before Winter*, 331–32.

3. Taken from a message given on "Back to the Bible Broadcast."

4. Joseph Shore in Lloyd Cory, *Quotable Questions* (Wheaton: Victor, 1985), 55.

5. Geoff Colvin, *Talent Is Overrated* (New York: Portfolio Hardcover, 2008).

6. Ibid., 67–68.

7. Dana Foundation, *Cerebrum 2008, Emerging Ideas in Brain Science* (New York: Dano Press, 2008), 191–93.

8. Charles R. Swindoll, *Living Above the Level of Mediocrity* (Dallas: Word, 1987), 94–95.

9. Lloyd John Ogilvie, *God's Will in Your Life* (Eugene, OR: Harvest House, 1982), 144–45.

10. Gary Kinnaman and Richard Jacobs, *Seeing in the Dark* (Grand Rapids: Bethany, 2006), 130.

CHAPTER 7 Knocking Out Toxic Self-Talk . . . for Good!

1. Asher, *Brainswitching*, adapted, 188.

2. Hart, *Habits of the Mind*, 170.

3. Ibid., 162–72.

4. Ibid., 39.

5. Ibid., 38–39.

CHAPTER 8 Disarming Toxic Weapons in Your Marriage

1. *Webster's New World College Dictionary*, 3rd ed., s.v. "slander."

2. Paul Coleman, *The Forgiving Marriage* (Columbus, OH: McGraw-Hill, 1989).

3. Bernstein and Magee, *Why Can't You Read My Mind?*, 41.

4. Wright, *Dad-Shaped Hole*, 51.

5. Ibid., 142.

6. Aaron T. Beck, *Love Is Never Enough* (New York: Harper & Row, 1988), adapted, 207–8.

CHAPTER 9 Dousing "Hot" Thoughts

1. Clifford Notarius and Howard Markman, *We Can Work It Out* (New York: Putnam's Sons, 1998), 137–41.

2. Bernstein and Magee, *Why Can't You Read My Mind?*, 45–46.

3. Notarius and Markman, *We Can Work It Out*, 144–45.

4. Lynn Clark, *SOS Help for Emotions* (Bowling Green, KY: SOS Programs, 2002), adapted, 73.

5. Gary Emery, *A New Beginning: How You Can Change Your Thoughts through Cognitive Therapy* (New York: Simon & Schuster, 1981), adapted, 54.

CHAPTER 10 Emotions and Your Thoughts

1. Loren Fischer, *Highway to Dynamic Living*.

2. Dorothy Finkelhor, *How to Make Your Emotions Work for You* (Berkley: Medallion Books, 1973), 23–24.

3. Willard, *Renovation of the Heart*, 117.

4. Gary Oliver, *Real Men Have Feelings Too* (Chicago: Moody, 1993), 61.

5. Penelope Russianoff, *When Am I Going to Be Happy?: How to Break the Emotional Bad Habits That Make You Miserable* (New York: Bantam, 1988).

6. Ibid., adapted, 50–52.

7. Oliver, *Real Men*, 136–37.

8. Gary Hankins with Carol Hankins, *Prescription for Anger* (New York: Warner, 1988), adapted, 131, 197–200.

9. Ibid., 26.

10. Sidney Simon and Suzanne Simon, *Forgiveness* (New York: Warner, 1991), 75–76.

CHAPTER 11 Your Thoughts, Worry, and Depression

1. Archibald Hart, *The Anxiety Cure* (Nashville: Word, 1998), 18–20.

2. Kinnaman and Jacobs, *Seeing in the Dark*, 74–75.

3. James R. Beck and David T. Moore, *Helping Worriers* (Grand Rapids: Baker, 1994), adapted, 90.

4. Hart, *Anxiety Cure*, 156.

5. Beck and Moore, *Helping Worriers*, 51.

6. Edward Hallowell, *Worry* (New York: Pantheon, 1993).

7. Williams et al., *Mindful Way*, 23.

8. Stephen Ilardi, *The Depression Cure* (Cambridge, MA: DeCapo Lifelong Books, 2009), adapted, 93.

9. Ibid., adapted, 101–2.

10. Gregory Lantz with Ann McMurray, *Moving Beyond Depression* (Colorado Springs: Shaw, 2003), 35–36.

11. Ilardi, *Depression Cure*, 41.

12. Curtiss, *BrainSwitch*, adapted, 36, 50, 54–55, 60, 93, 118, 126, 148, 155, 168–172.

13. Ibid.

14. Williams et al., *Mindful Way*, 46–47.

CHAPTER 12 New Thoughts

1. Dennis Kinlaw, *The Mind of Christ* (Nappanee, IN: Francis Asbury Press, 1998), 14–15.

2. T. W. Hunt, *The Mind of Christ* (Nashville: Broadman & Holman, 1993), adapted, 8–12.

3. Ibid., 12.

4. Toler, *ReThink Your Life*, 57.

5. Ibid., 32–33.

6. Terence J. Sandbek, Patrick W. Philbrick, Letha Dawson Scanzoni, and Libby Nicholson, *The Worry Free Life* (Sacramento, CA: Green Valley Publishing, 2008), 137–38.

7. Ibid., adapted, 136–41.

H. Norman Wright is a licensed marriage, family, and child therapist, as well as a certified trauma specialist. The author of more than eighty books, Wright is on the faculty of Talbot Graduate School of Theology and conducts seminars on many subjects, including marriage enrichment, parenting, and grief recovery. His current focus is in crisis and trauma counseling and critical incident debriefings within the wider community.

Are you hampered by the baggage from your past?

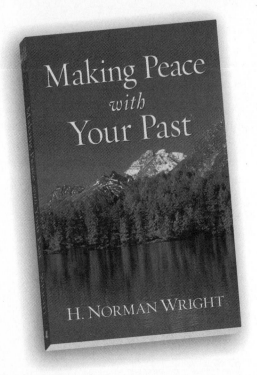

Dr. Wright shows you how to unlock past hurts, confront emotional scars, and resolve negative feelings. This book will help you understand who you are, who is responsible for your character, and how you can let go of the things of the past in order to live with confidence and enthusiasm.